The Fruit-Filled Life

Mónica E. Mastronardi de Fernández

Church of the Nazarene
Mesoamerica Region

Level C - Growing in Holiness
Youth/Adults

Title: The Fruit-filled Life

Book of "Discipleship ABCDE"
Level C - Growing in Holiness
Series: Full of the Holy Spirit
Study Guide for Youth/Adults

Author: Mónica Mastronardi de Fernández
Editor: Dr. Mónica Mastronardi de Fernández
Reviser: Rubén E. Fernández

Material produced by: Church of the Nazarene, Mesoamerica Region
Discipleship Ministries
www.Discipleship.MesoamericaRegion.org
www.SdmiResources.MesoamericaRegion.org

Copyright © 2020 - All rights reserved

ISBN: 978-1-63580-175-0

It's permitted to reproduce this material if not for commercial gain, only for use for discipleship in local churches.

All quotes are taken from the New International Version (NIV) bible by the
International Bible Society, unless indicated otherwise.

Design: Juan Manuel Fernández (www.betterworldagency.com)
Front cover image by Trey Jones

Cover images used by permission under the license of Common Good (Abstracto/Quito)

Printed in Guatemala

Contents

Presentation

Discipleship ABCDE

How Do I Use This Book?

Lesson 1 - Disciples are Known by Their Fruit *12*

Lesson 2 - The Fruit of the Spirit and the Works of the Flesh *22*

Lesson 3 - The Fruit of the Spirit is Love *32*

Lesson 4 - Love that Produces Joy *42*

Lesson 5 - Love that Makes Us Instruments of Peace *54*

Lesson 6 - Love that Produces Unlimited Patience *66*

Lesson 7 - Love Shown in Solidarity to Others *76*

Lesson 8 - Goodness: Proactive Love *88*

Lesson 9 - Love that Perseveres *98*

Lesson 10 - Love that Produces Meekness *110*

Lesson 11 - Love that Produces a Balanced Life *120*

Lesson 12 - The Fruit of the Spirit in the Church *128*

Lesson 13 - Exercising the Gifts and Fruit of the Spirit *136*

Presentation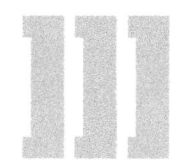

The Christian's life is a continuous walk in the process of discipleship, in which our whole being is being transformed to become like Jesus Christ through the Holy Spirit's work in us. All of us who have been "born again" need to participate in this process of formation so that we can become mature and holy Christians in all areas of our lives.

This volume titled: The Fruit-Filled Life, is the third of a three-volume series that completes the basic studies for level C of the ABCDE Discipleship Plan of the Church of the Nazarene in the Mesoamerica Region. The series is called: Filled with the Spirit and covers 9 months of studies. Each book contains 13 discipleship lessons focused on the consolidation and growth needs of people who have recently been incorporated into local church membership.

These lessons have been written with the thoughtful discipler/teacher in mind, and offers guidelines about how the teacher should instruct the group of new members in such a way that the class is interesting, dynamic and applicable to their lives. These books present the doctrine and practice of the life of holiness in simple practical language, and at the same time connect with the ideas of the contemporary world. The holy life is studied emphasizing:

A. The natural and progressive changes that are produced in the Christian, as a result of the action of the Holy Spirit in one's life; changes that are observable not only by oneself, but by all those around him or her.

B. The life full of the love of God as an indispensable requirement to serve the Lord and our fellow man.

C. The progressive and total transformation of the life of believers as we become more and more like Jesus Christ.

This third book in the series: The Fruit-Filled Life, has the purpose of providing tools to the believer to cultivate the fruit of the Holy Spirit in their life and thus personally experience the fullness of God's love and at the same time, be a light reflecting that love full of grace, righteousness, and truth in your home, in your church and in society. Each lesson presents a new opportunity for God to continue to work and transform each disciple so that we all might become more like Jesus in the way we think, in our emotions, and lifestyle, through bible studies, examples and illustrations, self-assessment exercises, reflection, as well as the opportunity to set new goals for spiritual growth.

It's my prayer that these lessons will help the members of our churches to understand and live more in the holy lifestyle of our beloved Savior, Jesus Christ.

Rev. Monte Cyr
Discipleship Ministries Coordinator
Mesoamerica Region

What is Discipleship ABCDE?

In the Church of the Nazarene, we believe that making disciples in the image of Christ in the nations is the foundation of the mission of the Church and the primary responsibility of the leadership (Ephesians 4:7-16). The work of discipleship is continuous and dynamic, that is to say, the disciple is never to cease growing more like the Lord. This process of growth, when it's healthy, occurs in all dimensions: as individuals (spiritual growth), in the corporate dimension (becoming part of the congregation), as well as in holiness of life (progressively becoming more like Jesus Christ), as well as in a life invested in service to God and others.

The ABCDE Discipleship Plan has been designed to contribute to the comprehensive formation of members of the churches of the Nazarene in the Mesoamerica Region. We have published materials to cover all discipleship levels. The three books in The Spirit-filled Life series correspond to the basic series for Level C, and have been designed for those who have gone through previous levels of discipleship with New Life in Christ materials and Keys to Abundant Christian Living (Level B1 and B2), and have been incorporated into church membership.

The books of the series Filled with the Spirit are intended to guide the new member of the church to become like Jesus Christ. As each person advances in the study of these materials, he or she will be discovering those areas of their lives that Jesus Christ wants to transform, so that the Holy Spirit of love can fill their whole being. The Spirit-filled life is the indispensable prerequisite to enable every son or daughter of God to realize the special plan that God has for his/her life.

Dr. Mónica Mastronardi de Fernández
General Editor ABCDE Discipleship
Church of the Nazarene - Mesoamerica Region

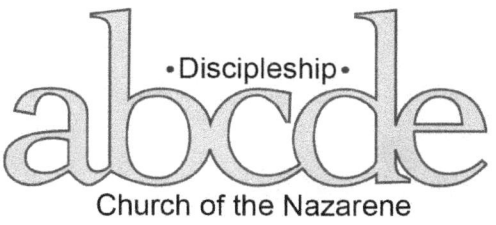

Discipleship abcde
Church of the Nazarene

Level A | Approach
Evangelism.

Level B | Baptism and Membership
Discipleship for New Believers.

Level C | Continued Growth in Holiness
"Filled With the Spirit" Discipleship.

Level D1 — Ministry Development
School of Leadership.

Level D2 — Professional Development
Specialized Training through Theological Institutions.

Level E | Education for Life and Service
Wholistic Growth in Christlikeness.
Christlike Disciples Making Christlike Disciples

Prevenient Grace — Saving Grace — Sanctifying Grace

"A Journey of Grace"

How to use this Book

This book belongs to a series of three volumes on the theme "Filled with the Spirit." The books are designed to be studied in the following order:

1. The Spirit-filled life
2. The Mind refocused on Christ
3. The Fruit-filled life

The purpose of this series is to help the members of the churches of the Nazarene get to know the biblical teaching on the holy life and to put what they are learning into practice in their daily lives in order to grow in their likeness to Jesus Christ.

How much time is needed to cover the study of the book?

Each book contains 13 lessons. If you guide them to study one lesson per week, the entire study will last three months. Sometimes groups prefer to go slower and spend two weeks studying each lesson. In that case, the study of the book will take 26 weeks (about six months). Remember that the goal of discipleship is not about rushing through to complete a book, but that group members might grow in the likeness of Jesus Christ. And in order to grow, they need to study, understand, and apply these new teachings to their lives. So planning the time for the study of each lesson in advance is very important, to ensure the disciples' progressive learning.

By their didactic design, the books can be used in different modalities; either for one-on-one discipleship, in small groups or in classes of more people.

What do the lessons contain?

Each lesson contains the following:

- Objectives: formulation of the learning goals that the students are expected to achieve at the end of the study of each lesson.
- Resources: ideas are included to illustrate and make learning more interesting.
- Introduction: the subject of study is introduced in an interesting way to awaken the interest and participation of students.
- Bible study: this is the most extensive section since it's the development of the contents of the lesson. These lessons have been written with the book as a teaching agent in mind, so its content is expressed in dynamic, simple language and makes connection with the ideas of the contemporary world. This section includes notes to the teacher about student participation in lesson development (Bible reading, questions, exercises from the Work Sheet).

- Summary of the main teaching of the passages studied: at the end of the lesson a small summary is provided. This summary is very useful to use at the end of the class as a closing point and/or the beginning of the next session to remember the topics discussed.
- Definition of Key Terms: This section is intended to clarify or broaden the meaning of some of the terms contained in the lesson.
- Work sheets: This page can be found and copied for the students, although ideally each student should have their own copy of the study booklet. As the lesson progresses, both individual and group learning activities related to the topic will be included.
- Recommended Readings: At the end of the Work Sheets, there are bible readings relative to the topics studied. Both teacher and students are encouraged to use these verses in their devotions during the week.

What is the role of the student?

The student is responsible for:

1. Acquiring the book and studying each lesson before each class. This is recommended, depending on the possibilities of each church.

2. Attend classes promptly.

3. Participate in class activities by completing the Work Sheets.

4. Apply the teachings of the Bible to their daily lives.

What is the role of the teacher?

1. Prepare the class session beforehand, studying the content of the lesson and scheduling the use of class time. The teacher needs to study the lesson with a Bible and a dictionary available for consultation. Pay attention to the vocabulary used in the lessons, and explain in simple words what might be difficult for the students to understand.

2. The teacher should allow the Holy Spirit to transform his/her own life and put into practice any new teaching, in order to be an example to the students.

3. Pray every day so that the objectives of each lesson becomes a reality in the lives of the disciples. Pray for the specific needs of each one of them.

4. Bring extra copies of the Work Sheet when students don't have a copy of the book. Complete the activities to become familiar with the exercises.

5. Prepare the teaching resources well in advance.

6. Connect with disciples outside of class. These lessons are intended to enable people to have transforming experiences which will help them to become more like Christ. Share with them and encourage them to apply to their lives what they are learning, and make sure they know that you're there to help them.

How to teach a class?

The lesson should last from between 90 to 120 minutes depending on the number of students and their participation. It's recommended that students read the lesson in advance so that they will have more time in class for discussion and application of the teachings.

In the course of the lesson, directions for the activities in which the students participate are included, such as Bible readings, discussion questions, or exercises to complete in the Work Sheet.

Whether you choose to study one lesson per week or one lesson in two weeks, we recommend that you distribute the time as follows (for 90 minutes of class):

- 5 minutes: welcome, review the theme and main points from the previous lesson, and prayer together.
- 10 minutes: introduction to the lesson topic.
- 60 minutes: lesson development. Use visual aids such as blackboard, graphics, drawings, objects, pictures, among others, and encourage student participation through questions or assigning students to take part in the lesson, etc.
- 10 minutes: share testimonies and a time of prayer for the issues raised in the lesson (challenges, personal situations, problems, goals, gratitude, among others).
- 5 minutes: announcements and farewell.

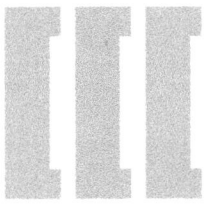

Disciples are Known by Their Fruit
Lesson 1

 ### Lesson Objectives

That the students might...

- **Understand** that the Spirit-filled life is fruitful.
- **Reflect** on the consequences of living an unproductive Christian life.
- **Reject** the temptation to adopt an uncommitted Christian life-style.
- **Choose** to walk along the Christian path in a close relationship of love with the Lord.

 ### Visual Aids

- Tender and flexible branches of a fruit tree, such as lemon or mango or some other tree, even better with flowers or small fruit.
- Grapes, raisins or grape juice.

Introduction

In the first book of this discipleship series - The Spirit-Filled Life, we studied the fact that the Christian life is one of constant growth in which we learn step by step to live like Christ. In the second book - The Mind Refocused on Christ, we learned that this development implies being molded into the likeness of Christ in our minds, in our affections (heart) and in our behavior. In this book, we're going to study about how to live a fruitful life as disciples of Jesus Christ.

In the Bible, we find a lot of teaching about how to live a profitable Christian life, not only for ourselves, but also so that our lives become a source of blessing to others, thus contributing to the extension of God's Kingdom.

Jesus was a very skilled teacher in the use of parables, through which he transmitted to his listeners lessons based on real life situations which they could easily relate to. After listening to him, they could continue to meditate on the implications of these teachings for their lives. To achieve this purpose, Jesus chose visual images that his audiences knew very well.

This revolutionary method of teaching was very effective for a population in rural areas where only three percent could read and write. Most of the education was transmitted from the parents to the children orally, and through observation and imitation. The teaching of reading and writing was carried out in the synagogue schools, where only boys attended between the ages of 5 and 15, to study the books of the Old Testament, especially the five books of the Pentateuch. In commercial cities, the percentage of literacy could reach 15 percent.

The illustrations that Jesus chose weren't taken at random, but carefully selected so that the teaching could be fixed in his audiences' memories. Most of the time, Jesus didn't explain the meaning of these examples, but he hoped that his listeners would discover every detail by meditating again and again on what they had heard. On some occasions, his listeners, not being accustomed to his innovative teaching methods, asked the Master to explain the meaning because they failed to make the connection to their lives (for example with the parable of the sower and the wheat and the tares - John 13: 1-43). On those occasions, with great love and patience, Jesus helped them understand the meaning.

In this lesson, we'll analyze one of these word pictures that Jesus used in his teachings to reveal the principles that support the full life that Jesus expects his disciples to be able to lead. Jesus based this metaphor on plants or trees that produce food in the form of seeds and fruit.

Ask the students to read John 15:2 in unison.

 Show the twigs (small branches) to the class and ask the students to look at them, using their senses. They need to complete Worksheet Activity 1.

Jesus spoke of twigs like these. A twig is a tender and flexible branch of a plant, shrub or tree, where the fruit will develop. Let's see what this twig teaches us about how to be more productive disciples for God's kingdom.

The Fruit-Filled Life

# Bible Study

1. Nutrition and productivity

Jesus chose the vine plant, a plant that abounded in those days throughout the land of Palestine, so that his disciples could understand that the Christian life, far from being sterile, unproductive, idle or arid, must be fertile, profitable, fruitful and industrious.

||| Ask a student to read John 15:1-10. |||

We can learn a lot from this metaphor about the relationship of how disciples need to learn to depend on God the Father, the Son and the Holy Spirit. In this divine relationship, each party assumes well-defined responsibilities. The health of the vineyard requires teamwork. The metaphor also warns of the negative consequences that occur when one of the parties interrupts the relationship, and the multiple benefits received when all parts are connected together.

2. "I am the true vine"

Jesus had just instituted the Lord's Supper with his disciples; there may even have been in front of them on the table some cups and jugs with wine. As on other occasions, Jesus began with the statement: "I am." Each time he did this, he revealed aspects of his own divine nature and his work. Jesus also said that he was light (John 8:12), the door (10: 7), and the shepherd (John 10:11).

"I am" is the name by which God revealed himself to Moses in Exodus 3:13-14: *"Moses said to God, Suppose I go to the Israelites and say to them, 'The God of your fathers has sent me to you,' and they ask me, 'What is his name?' Then what shall I tell them?" God said to Moses, "I AM WHO I AM. This is what you are to say to the Israelites: 'I AM has sent me to you.'"*

On this occasion, Jesus affirms: "I am the true vine." Because of the Jews' knowledge of the books of the Old Testament, it was easy for them to relate the vine to the people of Israel. The prophets Isaiah, Jeremiah, Ezekiel and Hosea had already used this metaphor comparing Israel with a vineyard (Isaiah 5:1-7; Jeremiah 2:21; Ezekiel 15, 19:10; Hosea 10:1). The Jews were very proud of a great golden vineyard carved on the wall of the most holy place in the Temple of Jerusalem representing the nation of Israel. There were also coins that had the image of a vine. But when the prophets referred to Israel as a vine, they didn't do so to praise the nation for their faithfulness to the Lord and their accomplishments, but rather to point out that they weren't a vine of which God was proud.

The nation of Israel wasn't a genuine, real, true vine. It had been corrupted, adulterated and contaminated. Isaiah reproached them for having become a wild plant. Jeremiah told them that they had become the branch of a strange vine. Many Jews, and probably some of the disciples, thought that because they belonged to the Jewish people, they were automatically part of the vine of the only true God. But that wasn't true.

Jesus Christ is the only "genuine" vine whose fruit is trusted. He's the only vine that can bear "good fruit." As Jesus said on another occasion: *"'I am the way, the truth and the life,' Jesus replied. 'No one comes to the Father except through me'"* (John 14:6). So, the vineyard in this metaphor represents the authentic church, the new people that God is raising among all nations. Jesus Christ is the trunk that provides life to this vine. Every branch that's grafted onto another vine is destined for death.

○ Ask students to complete Worksheet Activity 2.

3. Unproductive branches

> **For this section, use the graphic, the productive vineyard, included in Activity 3 as a visual aid.**

The roles in the vineyard are well defined. For a vine to produce quality grapes, it needs a lot of care. God the Father is like the farmer who takes care of the health of the vineyard, making sure that the conditions of the soil, water and fertilizers favor the full development of the branches that sprout from the trunk.

In vineyards, the work is continuous, involving removing weeds, eliminating dead or diseased branches, fighting pests or insects, removing debris around the roots, etc. The ground must be perfectly clean. In Jesus' day, it was customary to build a wall around the vines or a watchtower to protect the vineyard from foxes and wild boars.

God the Father is the one who performs the pruning, cutting and cleaning the vineyard. The pruning work in Israel was done twice a year. In winter, the dead branches are cut, and in the spring, the useless sprouts or twigs that take away vitality and energy from the plant were cut away. Pruning is drastic; all branches that deprive the plant of its strength are cut and thrown away. Then when they're dry, they're burned.

In God's vineyard, unproductively is not acceptable. The only reason why there are branches on the vine is to produce grapes. The branches of the vine, once broken, have no use since they're soft wood and can't be used as firewood. In the New Testament, it also couldn't be used as an offering to use in the sacrifices of the Temple.

Jesus tells his disciples that whoever doesn't bear fruit will be cut off from the vine. Who is the Lord referring to with these words? He includes all those who profess to be Christians with their words, but don't show it in their lives and actions. There are people we listen to who try to convince us of their faith and their fidelity to Jesus Christ, but when we get to know them better, their lives disappoint us because they really aren't very different from the rest of the sinners in the world.

The life of the Christian who doesn't produce fruit won't end well; they're heading towards ruin. Everything that they've done during the process of discipleship will be lost, and probably there will be backsliding that may move them away from church, and they may even turn away from their faith. William Barclay says: *"A fundamental principle in the New Testament is that futility invites disaster."*

4. The productive branches will be cleaned

The productive branches are those that are attached to the trunk, receiving the necessary nutrients for their development, thus fulfilling the purpose for which they were designed by the Creator.

During the first three years when a new vineyard is planted, they don't allow production of fruit. In Jn.15:3, Jesus tells his disciples that they have already been cleansed. What the Master meant was that they had spent more than three years going through a process of discipleship where they had received Jesus' teaching in their hearts. Their lives had been transformed, they already knew how to keep close to Jesus and to live in obedience to the Word.

Staying united to Jesus Christ cleanses us (v:4), but not just in a moment, such as when we're forgiven of our sins or bad habits. A permanent process of cleansing will continue as a result of a relationship of fellowship with Jesus. No one can remain faithful to Jesus Christ without this continuous cleaning up process in their lives. The filth of sin must not be present in the life of Christ's disciple. The natural state of the life of a healthy Christian is one "free from sin."

In the vineyard, the productive branches are those that are attached to the trunk. Once the fruit is harvested, the vines are pruned and they continue to produce more fruit each year. It's a continuous cycle. In the first years of the plant, the branches that are pruned become thicker and stronger and more resistant. As the years go by, these branches change and their appearance becomes similar to the trunk. They no longer look like green and fragile stems, but they look the color of wood, as extensions of the main trunk. These are called branches. From these mature branches, other young twigs are born. So, a branch that previously only produced a cluster of grapes can now produce several bunches of grapes each season. At the same time, the clusters are bigger and the grapes too.

5. The function of the branches is to produce abundant fruit

In the valleys of Israel, when the weather was favorable, clusters of grapes were grown so large that two men were needed to support their weight. We can see this in the case of Joshua and the 12 spies. When they returned from their first exploration into the Promised Land of Canaan, they commented that: *"When they reached the Valley of Eshkol, they cut off a branch bearing a single cluster of grapes. Two of them carried it on a pole between them, along with some pomegranates and figs."* (Numbers 13:23).

In 1984, the Guinness World Records noted a cluster of grapes weighing 9.4 kg in Chile. In Israel, the clusters weigh an average of 4.5 and 5.5 kilos, but there are records of clusters that weigh between 12 and 20 kilos. A well maintained and pruned vine can remain alive for many years producing grapes. There was a famous vine in Jericho that was over 300 years old; its trunk was like a tree measuring 46 centimeters in diameter.

The fruit of the vine is very beneficial for our health. In Jesus' time, they ate grapes fresh or dried as raisins, and also 'stepped' on them to make wine. Today grapes, including their skins and seeds, are very valuable parts of our diet.

 **Distribute the grapes or raisins and while eating them, ask students to complete Worksheet Activities 4 and 5.**

The Fruit-Filled Life

6. Remaining in the Son is Rewarded

The main branch (Jesus) is responsible for providing nutrition to the entire plant, to keep it alive, flourishing and producing fruit. The branches (us) cannot bear fruit on their own; they need to be attached to the trunk of the vine. We could say that the fruit comes from the trunk of the vine, and the branches are the vehicle by which that sap can produce grapes.

In John 15: 9 and 10, Jesus places great emphasis on the disciples remaining "in my love." This insistence was based on his own personal experience of intimate relationship with his Father and the Holy Spirit. Jesus' close relationship of love and obedience with the Father was the source that nurtured his life and his ministry.

Throughout his service on this earth, Jesus remained in unity with his Father, and the presence of the Holy Spirit was evident in his life. The fruit of this loving relationship between the Father and the Son were more than abundant. People could see this at all times and in everything he did; He was full of grace and truth. The love of the Father was evident in the life and deeds of Jesus.

When we remain united to Jesus Christ, we can experience and feel firsthand all the love that the Father has for each of us, and it becomes natural for us to respond to that love, loving the Lord our God with all our being.

What does it mean for us today to remain in the vine? For Christians, our relationship with Christ must be the most important of all. We must keep in touch with Him constantly, but also in intimate and special moments every day. As in every relationship, it must be mutual, it must go both ways. Jesus cannot cultivate a relationship with us if we don't cooperate.

Instruct students to do Worksheet Activity 6.

To remain in Jesus is to keep him in our lives every day and allow him to be part of everything we do. When we cultivate such a relationship with Jesus, we receive great benefits. Just as the branch receives sustenance from the trunk of the vine, our life receives constant strength from Jesus, spiritual energy that we can invest in service to others.

By remaining in Jesus, his love flows through us and impacts the lives of other people. The actions of selfless love of Jesus' disciples provoke gratitude and curiosity in those who see and receive them. People begin to wonder ... why do they do this? Why are they kind? Why aren't they selfish like other people? And when these people understand that it's Jesus who sends us and inspires us to do these good works for others, they turn their thoughts to God. The love of God in action moves hearts and turns people to God who want to be disciples of Jesus.

Finish the class by completing Worksheet Activity 7.

Definition of Key Terms

- **Branch:** a part of a tree which grows out from the trunk or from a bough (John 15:2).
- **Remain:** The Greek verb 'meno', remain, is widely used in the New Testament. Its means to stay, last, continue, dwell, endure, persist, retain and live. In the metaphor of the vine it's used in the sense of staying close to Jesus, being faithful to Jesus continuously, without interruptions.
- **Vine branch/cane/shoot:** It's a long, flexible and knotty branch of the vine from which sprout the leaves and bunches of grapes.

Summary

The metaphor of the vine teaches us that Jesus' disciples need to keep in a close relationship with him to bear much fruit for the kingdom of God. As disciples, our purpose is to produce fruit in abundance, but this is not possible if our life doesn't receive the nutrients from the source of life, Jesus Christ. Living the Christian life in a fruitful way is not an option, but a lifestyle that's characteristic of our new nature as sons and daughters of God. The branches that become independent (detached) from the vine and those that are attached but without fruit, will be cut and discarded so that the tree can concentrate all its resources on the productive branches. There's nothing that does more harm to the church than those who claim to be Christians with their mouths, but deny it with their deeds.

 **Worksheet**

ACTIVITY 1
Look at the branches and answer the following questions:

1. Why do trees and plants bear fruit and seeds?
   _____

2. What would be the consequences for mankind if trees and plants ceased to fulfill this function?
   _____

3. What characteristics must a plant meet to bear "good" fruit?
   _____

4. If only the tender branches bear fruit, what is the purpose of the rest of the plant?
   _____

ACTIVITY 2
What are the false vines that some people cling to in your context? Mark those things with an X in the following list:

__ Being of Jewish blood or practice the Jewish religion

__ Virgin Mary and other saints

__ Buddhism

__ Islamism

__ Mormonism

__ Witchcraft / Santeria

__ Indigenous religions

__ Church leader

__ Being a member of the "x" church

__ Being a descendant of faithful Christians

__ Political ideology

__ Political leader

__ Other…

Worksheet - Lesson 1

ACTIVITY 3
Graphic: The Productive Vineyard

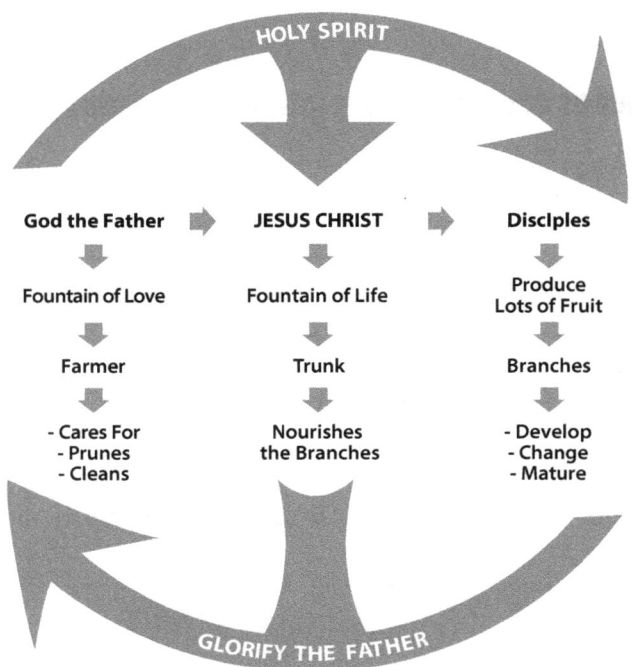

ACTIVITY 4
The fruit of the vine has been greatly appreciated since ancient times. The oldest vineyard on record is the one Noah planted. Today science continues to discover many of the benefits that eating grapes brings to our health. The following list includes some of the benefits that this wonderful fruit can bring to our integral health. Point out those health problems for which it would be good to include grapes more often in your diet:

Powerful antioxidant

Purifies the blood

Avoid fluid retention (diuretic)

Beautifies skin and hair

Prevents hypertension

Keeps arteries and veins healthy

Prevents the formation of cataracts in eyes

Fights bacteria and viruses (Vitamin C)

Strengthens bones, fights arthritis and rheumatism (Vitamins K, B-1)

Cleanses the intestines and prevents constipation (laxative)

The skin of grapes helps prevent cancer

Heart health

Prevents and improves diabetes

Fights anemia

Worksheet - Lesson 1

ACTIVITY 5
Make a graphic or drawing that represents how you imagine your fruitful career will be as a disciple of Jesus from today until the end of your life.

ACTIVITY 6
Reflect on the following sentences and then answer: Do I treat Jesus as my main relationship or as someone I look to from time to time? What would I do with a friend who treats me this way?

"Some Christians treat Jesus as if he were a 'Facebook' friend. At times we respond to messages from friends and at times we ignore them. At the beginning, we sent photos, birthday cards, shared what we were doing, asked them for advice before making decisions, asked for prayer requests ... But then, over time, we only write to our friend when we're having a problem or need advice or ask for help because we lack money or are sick."

_____

_____

_____

ACTIVITY 7
Work in groups. Think of an effective illustration to teach about the fruitful life that Jesus expects from his disciple in your context. Consider that some images may be effective in rural areas, but not so much for people living in big cities. Propose several ideas and choose the one that best conveys the principles of a productive Christian life. At the end, share your group's top idea with the rest of the class.

_____

_____

_____

_____

Worksheet - Lesson 1

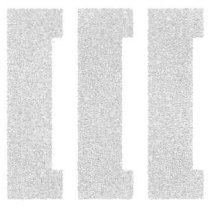

The Fruit of the Spirit and the Works of the Flesh
Lesson 2

 **Lesson Objectives**

That the students might...

- **Evaluate** if their life represents the 'good tree' or the 'bad tree', of the lesson.
- **Identify** the works of the flesh produced by the bad tree.
- **Understand** that those who produce only good fruit are truly God's sons and daughters.
- **Renounce** non-Christian values they treasure in their lives.

 **Visual Aids**

- Pictures of trees with their own fruit and seeds.
- A drawing of a large tree on the board (see the model in activity 3).
- Cardboard cut-outs of fruit shapes. They must be a good size and be placed on the tree that will be drawn on the board.
- Markers for students to write the name of the fruit on the cardboard clippings.
- Clear tape or masking tape to place the fruit on the tree.

Introduction

The gospels of Luke and Matthew narrate another metaphor that Jesus used about trees. This time he compared the fruit that comes from good trees and bad trees. Jesus' teaching leads us to reflect on a very important issue that deals with the kind of life that's acceptable to God.

In the society around us, there's a lot of confusion about where the boundaries exist between good and evil, between what is pure and what is contaminated, and between right and wrong. Every day the television and the newspapers talk about corruption and lack of integrity. But many of us ignore the depth of the problem. Corruption is not a problem only for political leaders, or for those who manage public or company funds. Today, acts of corruption have spread throughout society, and are common in families, in companies, in schools, and we could say that they have become part of the culture.

 Ask students to complete Worksheet Activity 1.

Bible Study

1. THERE ARE ONLY TWO TYPES OF TREES

Ask two students to read both stories of this metaphor in Matthew 7:15-20 and Luke 6:43-44.

This metaphor is found within the Sermon on the Mount that covers chapters 5, 6 and 7 of the Gospel according to Matthew. In this section of the message, Jesus referred to the false prophets who, although they were dressed as sheep, were actually wolves that left death and destruction in their wake.

In Israel, prophets dressed in ways that distinguished them: Elijah wore a sheepskin robe (1 Kings 19: 13,19). The prophet Zacharias warned that there were those who wore the prophet's mantle, but they were liars and they could not be trusted, for they didn't live as true prophets (Zechariah 13: 4).

In the days of the Early Church, the prophetic ministry was present in the form of itinerant preachers who visited the churches. Paul warned the Ephesian Christians to be careful about false prophets.

▌▌▌ Ask a student to read Acts 20:29. Then ask the class... How are the words of Jesus in Matthew 7:15 and those of Paul in this passage similar? ▐▐▐

As we see, the external aspect is not the best way to judge a person's character. We know that the image that a person projects doesn't always portray what that person really is. Dressing as a doctor doesn't make us doctors, wearing police clothes doesn't make us law enforcement officers, dressing as a pastor doesn't make us pastors, and so on. That's why the Master, in the metaphor of the vine and in this one about trees, affirms that the best way to know what a person is really like is by seeing their 'fruit.'

Jesus spoke of only two types of trees: bad ones and good ones. There are no more kinds of trees. There are no trees that bear good fruit and hide some bad fruit among their branches, nor bad trees that can bear good fruit.

This teaching of Jesus is radical and totally opposed to current ideas. Often in films, in soap operas and in the contemporary series, the lives of drug traffickers, thieves, murderers, deceivers, scammers and many others are represented. Although they are criminals and wicked, we're shown their good qualities, such as their love for their families or their partners. They also help the needy, etc. On the other hand, characters that appear as good people, such as pastors, parents, doctors, lawyers, police, among others who embrace very noble causes, are shown to have secret sins, are adulterers, abusers of minors, thieves, violent with their family, among others.

▌▌▌ Ask students to mention examples of movies, books, TV series and other programs that disseminate ideas like these for adults, youth and children. ▐▐▐

2. A BAD TREE BEARS BAD FRUIT

The bad tree is a corrupt tree, that is, perverted, bad, vicious, depraved, dishonest, corrupted. This tree represents the human heart full of evil. This is the natural state of the heart of all human beings who have not yet been cleansed of their sins by Jesus Christ. The only way we can get a pure heart is when God creates it within us. That's why the psalmist exclaimed: *"Create in me a pure heart, O God, and renew a steadfast spirit within me" (Psalm 51:10).*

This tree however, won't produce good fruit. The apostle Paul calls evil fruit "works of the flesh." We can see a list of some of these fruit in Galatians 5:19-21:19 *"The acts of the flesh are obvious: sexual immorality, impurity and debauchery; idolatry and witchcraft; hatred, discord, jealousy, fits of rage, selfish ambition, dissensions, factions and envy; drunkenness, orgies, and the like. I warn you, as I did before, that those who live like this will not inherit the kingdom of God."*

 **Do Worksheet Activity 2.**

▌▌▌ Distribute the pieces of paper with the fruit shapes for the students to write the names of the contemporary sins they wrote in Activity 2. Then ask the students to place the fruit on the tree you have drawn on the board. ▐▐▐

 **Ask students to complete Activity 3, copying the model from the board.**

Only God can change a bad heart into a good one. The Lord promised through the prophet Ezekiel that the Messiah would make it possible for the sons and daughters of God to have a new heart and be filled with the Holy Spirit: "I will give you a new heart and put a new spirit in you; I will remove from you your heart of stone and give you a heart of flesh" 36:26). A heart of stone is a bad heart, one that's not moved by the needs of others, one that's not obedient to the Word of God. We won't be able to bear good fruit for God with a heart of stone.

There are Christians who keep their hearts hard. We expect that after a time of attending church, our hearts will evolve into good hearts. These Christians cling to former ways and don't allow themselves to be transformed by God. They maintain bad things like pride, roots of bitterness, envy, hate and others that they have gotten used to. They get confused thinking that they can still serve God when their lives don't please God.

But these hidden desires in their heart come to light in their words and their actions. If they try continue to live this "double life", they will deceive themselves thinking that as long as they do a certain number of good things, their life will be acceptable to God.

> **Ask the class: Is it possible to serve in some church ministry as a leader in the church with an impure heart?**

Yes, it's possible to gain prestige for our ministry and have the admiration of others for our abilities. All this is possible to achieve, even though we're a 'bad tree.' But we must not confuse the projected image with the true identity of a person. We must not confuse either the appearance of the fruit with the quality of the fruit. How many of us have opened a nice looking avocado to find that it's black inside and have had to discard it? Or cut open a watermelon and as we eat it we realize that it doesn't have that sweet taste we expected?

3. THE GOOD TREE BEARS GOOD FRUIT

In the metaphor of the two trees, the fruit of the good tree are totally different from those of the bad tree, and this good fruit shows that the tree is good. From the fruit of this tree, we can sow seeds with the confidence that over time, we'll get another tree that will bear fruit of quality.

This good tree represents the Christian life which is whole, truthful, honest, upright, sincere, and patient. These people obey the Word of God, have new hearts given to them by God; hearts that are clean, pure and holy. Their lives reflect their commitment to God and His work all the time. At home, on the street, at work, at school, in the gym, wherever they are, others may notice that they are sons or daughters of God with pure hearts.

The true identity of Christians is shown by the quality of their fruit and seeds.

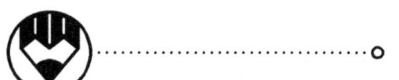 **Ask students to complete Activity 4.**

> **Show images of trees, their fruit and seeds to illustrate the next section.**

Each tree bears fruit according to its own nature. Apples are born from an apple tree, mangoes are harvested from the mango tree, the lemon tree produces lemons, etc. In nature, there are no pear trees that give figs or orange trees that give papayas. Likewise, each fruit gives seeds according to its species. This was the plan of the Creator (Genesis 1:11).

Jesus taught that obedience to God is always rewarded with more fruit. If we want to be a good tree, we need to start by surrendering to the Lord and asking Him to give us a new heart, one that's obedient to His Word, one that's pure and full of the Holy Spirit of God.

 Ask the students to complete Activity 5.

The Fruit-Filled Life

4. MY VALUES MAKE ME WHO I AM

In the parallel passage of Luke 6:45, Jesus says: *"A good man brings good things out of the good stored up in his heart, and an evil man brings evil things out of the evil stored up in his heart. For the mouth speaks what the heart is full of."*

Once again in Luke we see that the words that come out of our mouth are the product of what is in our hearts. Of course, we can control what we say and learn a spiritual and Christian language. But when we're under pressure, when emotions flow into words, when we say the first thing that comes to our heads, we can see the real product that comes out of our hearts.

Luke refers to a treasure that all human beings keep. What we choose to keep in that treasure is up to each one of us. But the type of person we are depends on this choice. Many times, the product of a bad heart comes to light at home, where parents, who in the church have a reputation for being good Christians, aren't good examples to their children, speak badly of the members and leaders of the church, speak harshly to their family, or even lie and cheat.

Jesus explains that if our treasure is good, our words and deeds will be good too. Our lives will be pleasing to God, and those around us will be blessed by our words and good deeds. But if our treasure is bad, it will lead us to deviate from God's will and seek to satisfy our own selfish desires, even harming other people.

In life, as in science, every effect has its cause. For example, if a person is aggressive or violent, there must be something in their heart that acts as the engine of that behavior. These treasures are the motives that drive us to act in a certain way. Today we call them principles or values.

We can understand values better when we think of a small seed, like the mustard seed that Jesus mentioned.

> **Ask a student to read Mark 4: 30-32. Then ask the class: How does this parable of the mustard seed resemble the metaphor of the vine and that of the good and bad trees?**

All people have values. We aren't born with these values but we learn them in our family, in school, in society, in the church, etc. For example, if we have the value of peace, we'll be peacemakers, we won't respond violently to violence. The opposite of values are anti-values. For example, the opposite of truth is the lie. When we learn an anti-value from an early age, we think it's part of our life. For example, if someone speaks untruths, we call them liars. It's as if lying was part of their nature, that they have no choice but to lie. But what really happens is that this person has not embraced the value of truth for his or her life.

The kingdom of God has its own values and they are all opposed to the anti-values of the world.

 **Ask students to complete Activity 6.**

The good news is that values and principles can be changed. It's never too late to learn new values. That's why it's so important to study the Word of God, because in it we can learn to embrace the values of the kingdom of God. Jesus' true disciples treasure the values of the kingdom of God in their hearts.

The most valuable person in a Christian's life is God himself. When God is the center of our hearts, He becomes our main treasure and the one we value most. The fruit of a life centered in God will produces love, because God who is love occupies the center of our being. Only a heart full of God's love will bear the fruit that the Lord expects from His disciples. This will be the subject of the next lesson.

 **Ask students to complete Activity 7.**

Definition of Key Terms

- **Avocado:** Edible fruit that's widely used all over the world.
- **Corruption:** When we say that something is corrupt, we affirm that its natural state has been altered by something that has been introduced, but that it's not typical of the thing or person being talked about. In organizations, it refers to the practices of people who use their functions to unethically obtain economic or other benefits. For human beings, living in sin is a state of corruption since we were created to live in holiness. Sin doesn't belong to our original nature. That's why, in the Bible, sin is related to an infectious disease that destroys our being and must be eradicated (Isaiah 53:5).
- **Works of the flesh:** They are the evil deeds and sinful behaviors that are characteristic of people who don't love God nor obey Him with their lives. This behavior causes harm and pain to the person himself and to those around him. Works of the flesh are opposed to the Fruit of the Spirit (Galatians 5:13-25).
- **Values:** These are the ideas or concepts that support our attitudes and our actions.

Summary

The type of person we're is not something that's predetermined by our genes and family background alone. Jesus teaches us that we can choose what kind of person we want to be. If we allow God to purify our hearts, and adopt God's plan as the most important value of our lives, then pure and holy fruit will result because of the love of God that dwells in us. But if we keep hearts of stone, ones that are rebellious to the will of God, and we hold onto values contrary to the kingdom of God, we won't be able to produce the good and pleasant fruit that God expects of us.

Worksheet

ACTIVITY 1
Indicate in the following list the things that you have done or do because they are things that people commonly do in their context.

__ Lie about the reason you're late for work.

__ Sneak in or get ahead in line.

__ Keep extra change at the supermarket.

__ Do not give my full tithe to the church.

__ Pay a bribe for a procedure.

__ Pass through a red light.

__ Buy "pirate" items (music, movies, clothes, computer programs).

__ Plug into others' electric cables or TV Cable.

__ Steal flowers or fruit from a garden or orchard.

__ Photocopy books with reserved rights instead of buying them.

__ Plagiarize text for college or university work.

__ Cheat on an exam.

ACTIVITY 2
In the following table you will find the fruit of the flesh from Galatians 5:19-21 listed. The first column is the phrase taken from the NIV and in parenthesis are modern definitions that might help to clarify the concept. In the right column, on each line write the name of sins that are present in your context and that are related or derived from the sins on the left.

Phrase take from the NIV	Contemporary versions of these sins
Sexual immorality	
Idolatry and witchcraft	
Impurity and debauchery (filthy and indecent actions)	
Hatred and discord (people become enemies and they fight)	
Jealousy and fits of rage	
Selfish ambition	
Factions (They separate into parties and groups)	
Envy	
Drunkenness and orgies (get drunk a lot, attend wild parties)	

Worksheet - Lesson 2

ACTIVITY 3
Draw the fruit of the bad tree.

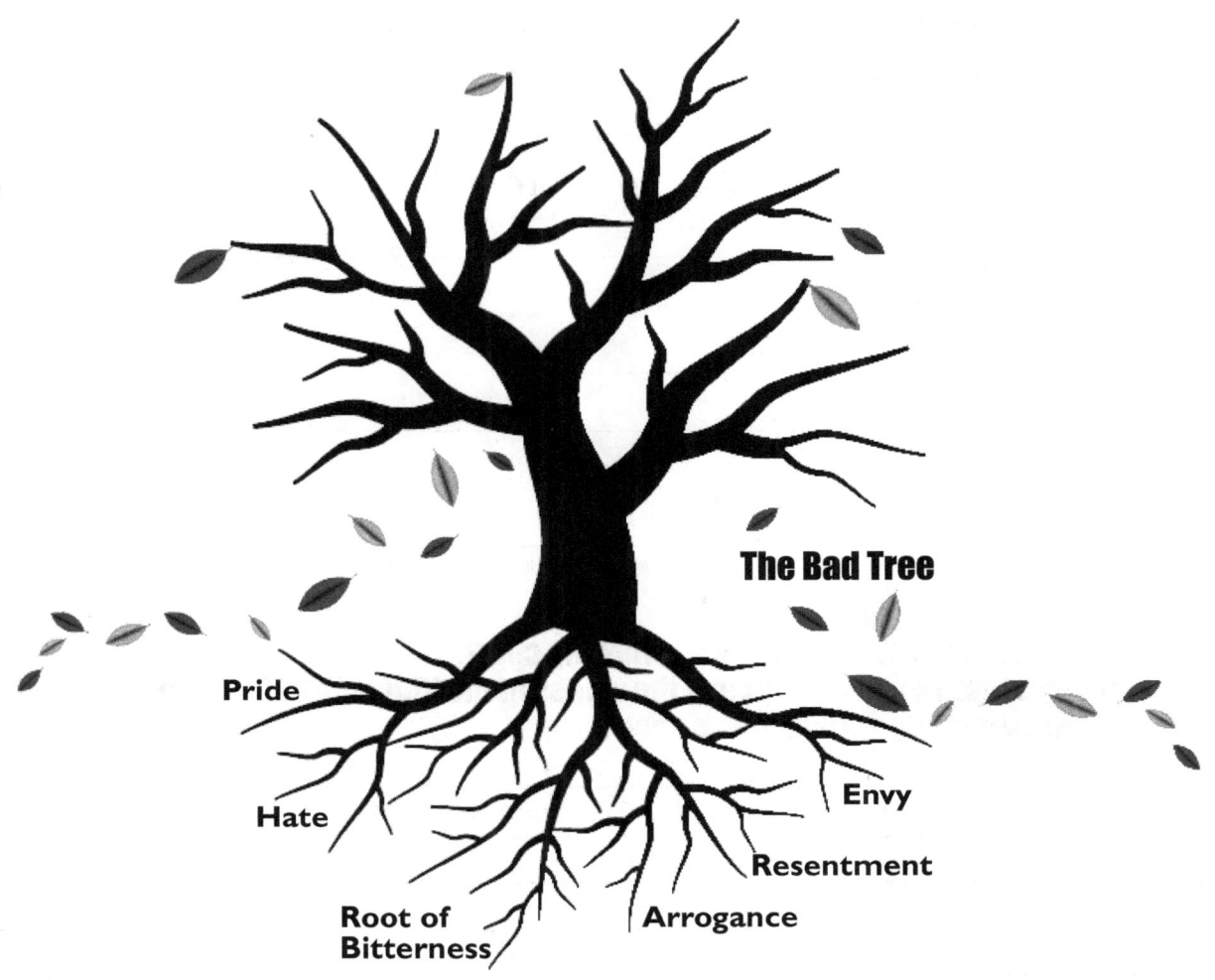

ACTIVITY 4
In groups of 2 to 3, answer the following questions:

a. According to the metaphor of the two trees, do you think that it's possible to know if a person is a good or bad Christian because of what they do?

b. Mention some bad deeds that some "Christians" do which invalidates their testimony (without giving names).

c. What are the good works that you have seen in some Christians you know?

ACTIVITY 5
Look in the Bible at the verses listed below and answer the questions.

a. John 12:24: What must happen to the grain of wheat to produce much fruit?

b. Galatians 5:24: What does an authentic Christian look like?

c. Revelation 20:12: Does God keep a record of our works? For what purpose?

d. Revelation 21:27: What will be the eternal destiny of bad trees?

e. Revelation 19: 6-8: What does the fine linen clothes that God's children will wear in Heaven represent?

_____

_____

_____

_____

_____

_____

ACTIVITY 6
**In groups of 3 or 4 students, complete the following chart.
In the left column there's a list of some of the values of the Kingdom of God. Write in the right column the corresponding anti-values in each case.**

Values of God's Kingdom	The World's Values
Simplicity	
Peace	
Solidarity	
Compassion	
Love	
Freedom	
Truth	
Service	
Life	
Purity / holiness	
Righteousness	
Sacrifice	
Faithfulness	
Brotherliness	

Worksheet - Lesson 2

ACTIVITY 7
Answer the following questions on your own:

a. Do you have the assurance that your life is a good tree? If your answer is no, what would you have to do to make your life a tree that bears good fruit?

b. What is the most important value in your life today?

c. Have you identified any anti-values present in your life? What one or ones?

d. What are the values of the kingdom of God that you need to embrace in your life?

_____
_____
_____
_____
_____
_____
_____
_____
_____
_____
_____
_____
_____
_____
_____
_____
_____
_____
_____
_____

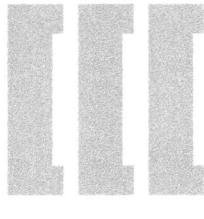

The Fruit of the Spirit is Love
Lesson 3

 **Lesson Objectives**

That the students might...

- **Identify** false forms of love
- **Know** the nature of God's love
- **Differentiate** between *eros* love and *agape* love
- **Make** the decision to work so that the Fruit of the Spirit develop in their lives.

 **Visual Aids**

- A citrus fruit such as a tangerine, an orange, or a grapefruit that can be separated into segments. The segments should be sufficient for the whole class.

Introduction

In the previous lessons we studied that Jesus' will is that his disciples bear good and abundant fruit. There are Christians who are confused about the kind of fruit Jesus was talking about. Some think that it refers to giving, others believe that it's about making more disciples, others that it's the service we provide in some church ministry, others that it's personal sacrifices, and there may even be some who think that it's about prospering economically in order to give more money for the work of God.

Everything we have mentioned can be done without having the true Fruit of the Spirit in our lives. But all these things, although good, can be done for the wrong reasons.

[[[Ask students to complete Worksheet Activity 1.]]]

As we saw in the previous lesson, we must pay attention to the motives that move us to do what we do. If we want to be trees that bear good fruit, our hearts must be filled with the holy love of God. In this lesson we're going to study that love that's the spiritual fruit that God expects of us, but as we'll see, it's not about any kind of love, but about a love that has all the good qualities of God's love.

Bible Study

1. GOD IS LOVE

Love is one of the most used words in our language. It's also a crucial word in the Bible. But there are so many different ways of understanding the concept of love that even for Christians it's difficult to understand what type of love the Bible is speaking about. The problem is that if we don't understand the biblical concept of love well, we won't be able to put it into practice as God expects us to.

In his first letter, the apostle John makes a revolutionary declaration for his time:

[[[Ask a student to read 1 John 4:8.]]]

Non-Christian religions don't follow what this verse states. John doesn't say, "God is loving," which would be correct if love were one of God's qualities. But it doesn't say this, but rather that love is the essence of who God is, His true nature. We cannot separate God from His love, nor can we understand what true love means if we don't know God.

The Fruit-Filled Life 33

The Bible says that God is generous, just, and wise because all these are characteristics of the Creator, but we shouldn't confuse characteristics with His very nature. At the same time, these characteristics and many others come from His love. Even those that may seem negative to us, like His anger, arise from His love.

In the creation of the original couple, God shaped the human race in His image and gave us His capacity to love. The fact that humans can love even without knowing God is a sign that love is part of our nature. But of that created capacity to love, there are hardly any vestiges left because it has been severely damaged and corrupted by sin.

▌▌▌ Ask a student to read 1 John 4:16 and ask the class: What is the only way in which people can put true love into practice? ▐▐▐

The statement of the apostle John is direct and clear. Love is "the fruit" that identifies us as authentic sons and daughters of God. But what sort of love is John talking about? Today there are so many different ways of understanding and living love that we need to clarify this issue.

   **Ask students to complete Activity 2.**

As we see, people have their own ideas about what love is and how we should love. Many Christians think of love as romantic love, which we see in movies and TV shows, and that affects the way we understand God's love and put it into practice.

Due to the prevailing confusion, we need to ask what is the true love of which the Bible speaks? To answer this question, we need to begin by investigating what God's love is like.

2. THE LOVE OF GOD

The Bible teaches that there are three main dimensions of God's love: justice, truth and grace, all of which are characteristic of his love.

▌▌▌ Draw the following graph on the board. ▐▐▐

The original Hebrew terms that are used for justice, truth and love have a slightly different meaning than in today's English. When the Bible affirms that God's love is shown in his justice, it doesn't refer to the ability to make an impartial and objective judgment according to the law, as we expect judges to do in courts today. Rather, God's justice refers to His true compassion for His creatures, a compassion that goes beyond the justice they should obtain according to the law. The justice of God is not cold or distant, but one that's moved by the compassionate love of God. In the Bible, justice is the compassionate love of God acting in defense of those most in need, going alongside those who suffer and don't receive fair treatment.

The love of God can be seen in His truth. The Bible teaches that God has all those characteristics of an authentic, complete person. The love of God is honest, truthful and holy. Because God loves us, He doesn't lie to us or deceive us. He doesn't use us for His selfish purposes, or exploit us, or have hidden agendas; He doesn't manipulate us.

The meaning of the Greek term *aletheia* - truth, implies revealing something that was hidden. For us from our human position, it's difficult to see the complete panorama and the causes behind the reality that surrounds us. But God's love is accompanied by His light, a light that penetrates all darkness and allows Him to see people and circumstances lovingly, discovering sin and revealing the most hidden intentions of hearts.

The love of God is also shown in the grace with which He accepts us, forgives us and cultivates a relationship with each of His children; He gives everything of Himself. His grace speaks to us of a love that embraces, redeems, includes and restores all those who wish to be part of His people.

Although the grace of God's love doesn't justify sin, it welcomes and forgives the sinners, accepting them into His family and helping them grow and develop. Jesus is the visible image of God's loving grace (John 1:14). He can see the potential of each person beyond their current situation, and he gives them hope.

 Ask students to complete Activity 3.

3. Love is the Fruit of the Spirit

Jesus spent much of his time with his disciples teaching them how they should love. This was the goal of many of his parables and miracles. Like the others Jews of their time, the disciples found it difficult to understand what kind of love Jesus expected from them. To make himself understood, Jesus used the metaphor of light. In Matthew 5:14 he said: *"I am the light of the world ..."* Thus, the disciples could understand that just as the moon reflects a light that wasn't its own, but that of the sun, they should reflect the light of Christ to others.

Later in his ministry Jesus told them that he would teach them a new commandment. The disciples were amazed because the Jewish law had 613 commandments and it was very difficult for any Jew to comply with all of them. But Jesus reassured them by explaining to them that this new commandment wasn't going to add another burden to the hard-working believer, but that it was the most important and essential of all the commandments and that it sums up all the others.

Ask a student to read John 13:34-35.

This was one more of the revolutionary teachings of Jesus. A commandment that in a nutshell summed up the desire of God's heart for all His children. Only those who were obedient to this commandment would be recognized as authentic disciples of Jesus. It seems a simple instruction to follow, but it's not. This is because we think that love is a feeling that will flow from our being, like when we fall in love. But John is not talking about that kind of love.

In the language of the New Testament, three words are used with very different meanings for love. For example, there is ***eros*** love, which refers to the desire to have something that you don't have.

It's a love which focuses on a person, as in the case of sexual desire, or on some object. Eros love is motivated by the desire to meet a personal need or feel complete. This love motivates the one who loves in this way to think about the object of his love and also to do works of love for the loved one.

The common way of thinking about love is that we must first have a feeling in order to have the will to think and do good things for the other person. The starting point of this love lies in the loving feelings that another person wakes up in us.

But the love of which Jesus speaks is *agape* love, which is a different kind of love. It doesn't have its origin in the object of desire, but in thinking about how can we show God's love to another person. It's a love that doesn't depend on our feelings. When the love of God has filled our heart, our mind shouldn't be governed by the feelings that others arouse in us, but by the loving way of thinking about our neighbors that we learned from Jesus Christ.

 Ask students to complete Activity 4.

That's why Jesus said that we must learn to love in a different way than the people around us.

Ask a student to read Matthew 5:46-47.

When we learn to practice agape love, we can even love our enemies (Matthew 5:44). But remember that we can only love like this when we're filled with the Holy Spirit. How then can this agape love of God dwell in our hearts and radiate to those around us?

If we try to show a true, just and graceful love like God's, in our own strength, we'll fail. It's only possible to love in this way when, like a mirror, we reflect the light of God to others.

Ask a student to read Romans 5:5.

The apostle tells us that when we're filled with the Holy Spirit, God's love is poured into our hearts. Love is the main "fruit" of the Spirit. It's a fruit that fills us with purpose and values on which to build our lives. This love is abundant, it spills over us, resulting in lives that will be filled with fruitfulness.

Ask a student to read Galatians 5:22-23.

 Ask students to complete Activity 4.

4. WE CAN LEARN TO LOVE

As we have seen, we need to learn a new way of loving, different from that of the world. The love of God is a gift for us, but it's also a duty that we must carry out every day.

Ask a student to read 1 Corinthians 14:1.

In this passage, the apostle Paul tells us how the Fruit of the Spirit, poured into our lives, becomes visible to those around us. In the Greek, the first thing mentioned is the most important thing.

The Fruit-Filled Life

▌▌▌ **Ask the class: What is the most important fruit that Paul mentions? How much more fruit is produced in the life of the Spirit-filled believer? Ask them to mention them. Then take out the citrus fruit and separate it into segments. Ask the class: How many segments does this fruit have? Then distribute the segments to be eaten and ask: What does the slice you're eating taste like? Why do they all have the same flavor?** ▌▌▌

Just like a citrus fruit, the Fruit of the Spirit has many segments but they all have the same distinctive taste of God's love.

 **Then ask students to complete Activity 5.**

God's children are responsible before the Lord to develop the Fruit of the Spirit He has given us. Learning to love with the love of God, full of grace, justice and truth, is a task that will take us the rest of our lives. In the following lessons, we'll learn to develop and put into practice this fruit of love in our daily lives.

 **Conclude the class by performing Activity 6.**

The Fruit-Filled Life

# Definition of Key Terms

- **Love:** *Agape* and *agapao* are the Greek terms that the New Testament uses to describe God's love for His Son (John 17:26), for the entire human race (John 3:16) and for those who believe in Jesus Christ (John 14:21). Those who follow Jesus must express this love to each other (John 13:34), and also to all other people (1 Thessalonians 3:12). This verb is used to describe the love that is the essential nature of God (1 John 4: 8). It's a constant and deep love that cares even for those who aren't deserving of that love. It's a love that's expressed in actions in favor of other people, as Jesus did by giving his life for our salvation (1 John 4: 9-10). This love is the distinctive practice of Christians in the New Testament. It's the love with which we must love God, responding to His love for us.

- **Fileo:** The Greek word *fileo* is used by the New Testament authors to describe affection between siblings, family members, friends or partners (John 3:35). This love arises from friendship (2 Samuel 1:26), and the greatest example of this love is Jesus Christ (John 15: 13-14). Jesus wants his followers to cultivate a deep friendship with him and also with each other.

- **Eros:** The term *eros* comes from Greek mythology: The god Eros caused the sexual impulses of human beings. The Romans had a god similar to what we call Cupids, who shot their arrows and made people fall in love. From this term is derived the word *eroticism*. In the Bible, *eros* love is the natural physical attraction between a man and a woman. It activates our hormones and is an important part in helping us follow God's command to join together in marriage and reproduce, to form a family. Eros love is blessed by God when practiced in the framework established by God, that is, within the marriage bond (Ephesians 5:25).

# Summary

The true sons and daughters of God are known by their fruit. When the Holy Spirit fills us, God's love floods our lives. This kind of love is different from the way we have learned to love in the world. It's not a love that originates in our desires or in our feelings or emotional needs, such as *eros* love. It doesn't depend on whether people like us or treat us well. It's a love that's born in a mind full of the love of God, that thinks in creative ways of demonstrating that just, true and compassionate love of the Creator to others. It's a love that acts on behalf of others, even those who hurt us.

 **Worksheet**

ACTIVITY 1
Indicate in the following list of selfish motivations which ones once prompted you to do something good.

__ Acquire fame or prestige

__ Earn money

__ Get along well with someone (my partner, my parents, my boss, etc.)

__ Barter with God, so that God grants me something

__ Add points to get to heaven

__ Be elected as a leader in the church

__ Obtain a certificate, medal or prize

__ Prevent being fired

__ Be accepted in a group

ACTIVITY 2
Do you know any person trapped in any of these "crooked" ways of loving?

__ Barter love: I love you if you love me.

__ Interested love: love in exchange for money, protection, goods.

__ Loving those who listen and agree with us

__ Conditional love: I will love you if you obey me.

__ Hard love: I mistreat you because I love you.

__ Dependent love: I love because I need you.

__ Unfaithful love: I love when I want to.

__ Forced love: I love because it's my duty.

__ Submissive love: I love because I'm afraid.

__ Love that submits: I love because I am weaker than you.

Worksheet - Lesson 3

ACTIVITY 3
Which of the dimensions of God's love is mentioned in these passages in the book of Psalms? Mark with an x in the corresponding box.

	Justice	Truth	Grace
Psalm 33:4-5			
Psalm 36:5-6			
Psalm 40:11-11			
Psalm 88:11-12			
Psalm 98:2-3			
Psalm 119:75-76			

ACTIVITY 4
Identify in the following flowcharts what kind of love it is and write it under each one.

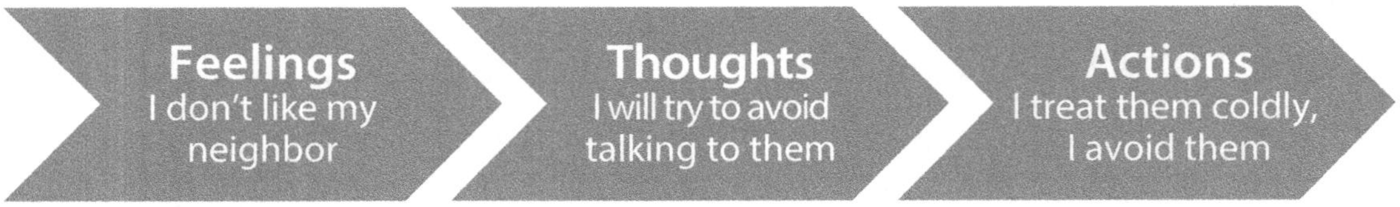

Feelings — I don't like my neighbor → **Thoughts** — I will try to avoid talking to them → **Actions** — I treat them coldly, I avoid them

Kind of Love _____

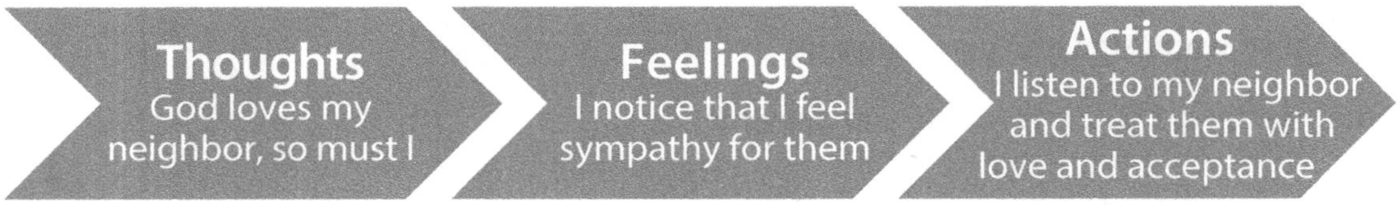

Thoughts — God loves my neighbor, so must I → **Feelings** — I notice that I feel sympathy for them → **Actions** — I listen to my neighbor and treat them with love and acceptance

Kind of Love _____

Worksheet - Lesson 3

ACTIVITY 5
In groups of 3 to 4 students, study the drawing of the good tree and its spiritual fruit. What differences do you find between this tree and the bad tree we studied in the previous lesson?

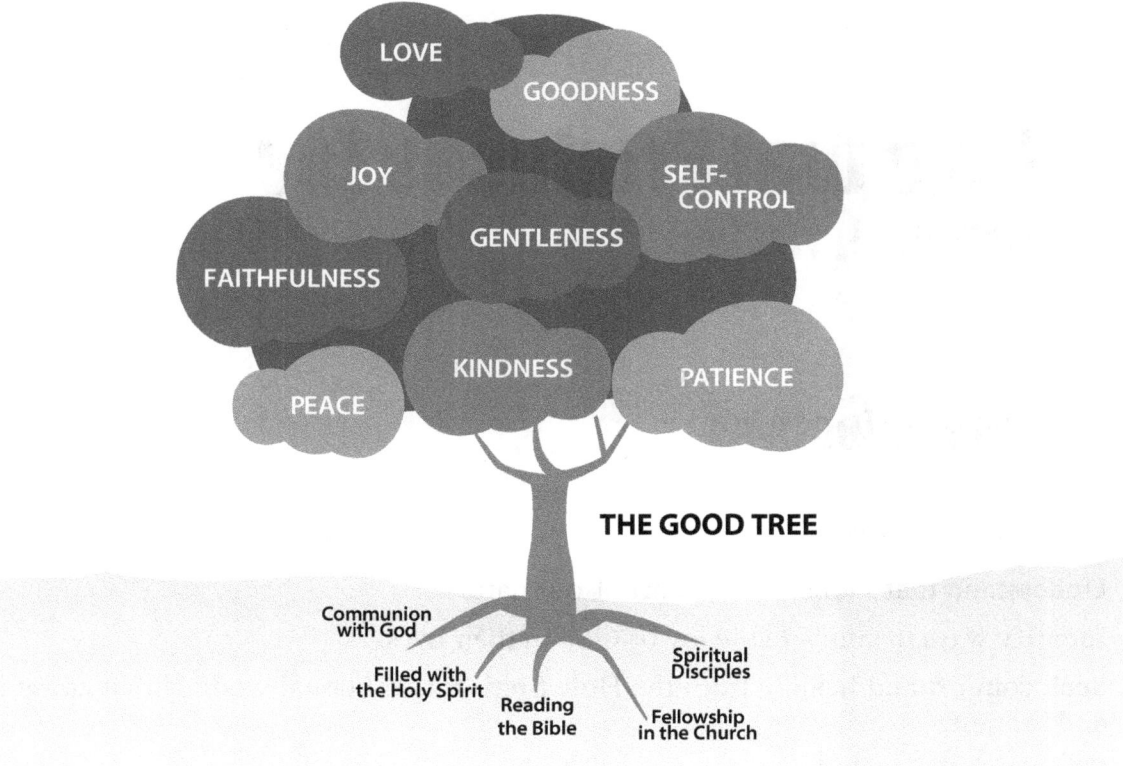

ACTIVITY 6
Answer the following questions and then write a personal prayer communicating your decision to God and asking him to help you reach the goals in which this book will guide you.

a. Should I change my way of loving others?

b. What do I need to do to learn to love as God loves?

c. Do I need to be filled with the Holy Spirit and the love of God?

d. Do I wholeheartedly want God to teach me to reflect to others his just, true and graceful love?

e. What changes will I start making this week in the way I show love to other people?

_____
_____
_____
_____
_____
_____

Worksheet - Lesson 3

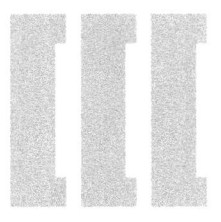

Love that Produces Joy
Lesson 4

Lesson Objectives

That the students might...

- **Understand** that sadness is not part of our nature.
- **Identify** ways to cultivate the joy of God in their lives.
- **Seek** comfort and healing from the Holy Spirit for emotional wounds that cause pain and sadness.
- **Choose** to live each day with a heart full of joy.

Visual Aids

- Photos or drawings of sad, serious faces and people crying.

Introduction

In the previous lesson we studied that the Fruit of the Holy Spirit is love, a love that's expressed in various ways in the life of a Christian. In this lesson, we'll discuss the theme of joy, the fruit that follows in Paul's list in his letter to the Galatians.

It's possible that in our community, people think that Christians are boring and sad people. Could there be believers who think the same?

Show the images of sad and serious people and ask the class: Why do you think some people have this idea that Christians are sad and bored? Can this idea be related to the image that some Christians project in our communities?

Nowhere in the Bible does it say that sadness should be one of the characteristics of the Christian life. On the contrary, joy is included as one of the eight qualities of God's love that others should be able to see in our lives.

Sadness is something nobody wants. Because of sadness, people become physically and mentally ill, and even their spirits can decay. Such is the case that sadness is diagnosed as a disease - depression. People suffering from sadness don't eat well, they neglect their personal hygiene and may even commit suicide or harm others or become murderers. Sad people have trouble keeping their friends and their partners.

 **Ask students to complete Activity 1.**

Some Christians accept living in a permanent state of sadness as if it were their calling and vocation. They embrace sadness as God's will for their lives. Some evangelical congregations even today impose rules on their members about not demonstrating joy in public, not attending parties organized by non-Christian people, dressing in clothing in the range of black or gray, the ladies covering their heads in worship, and they aren't supposed to clap in times of worship, among others.

In the Roman Catholic tradition, people are encouraged to impose sacrifices on themselves, such as walking to a cathedral barefoot or fasting for long periods. The belief is that these things please God and move Him to the point that He answers their prayers. Others believe that it's not possible for the Christian to be happy in this world; that the only happiness we can yearn for is when we'll have in eternal life.

Making sadness a way of life is like saying that God is the creator of suffering. But as we'll see in this lesson, the desire of God's heart is that his sons and daughters should be joyful, live happily in this life and spread happiness to those around us.

Bible Study

1. We are children of a cheerful father

Sadness makes us sick because it's not part of our nature. Some try to escape sadness by filling their lives with activities, but more often than not, when the rush of activity has gone, the sadness is still there. If we investigate the Internet search engines, we'll find that there are more than four million pages with advice about how to "escape" from sadness.

 Ask students to complete Activity 2.

God imprinted His joy on His creation. In the garden of Eden, sadness was something unknown. Adam and Eve lived happily until sin entered the human race. From there, we have searched for happiness by different means, such as alcohol, disorderly sex, the accumulation of material goods, occultism and false religions. But this sadness becomes greater when people see that their efforts are useless and that nothing can fill the emptiness inside.

The Bible affirms that God is our father, and because He is a good father, He wants his children to be happy. Our happiness is so important to God that He inspired the apostle Paul to mention it in second place in the Fruit of the Spirit, right after love.

Ask a student to read Zephaniah 3: 17-18. Then ask students: What promise does God make to his people through the prophet Zephaniah?

It's difficult for some of us to understand and accept that God loves us in this way, perhaps because our father or mother rejected us or mistreated us. Some of us have had absent parents, or very busy parents seeking their own happiness rather than taking care of their children. But God is not a father like that.

The promise that God made to the people of Israel through the prophet Zephaniah is also for each of us today. The love of God is powerful and can heal our wounds, renew our hearts and put His joy in each of His sons and daughters.

When we look at our life through God's eyes, we understand that He doesn't see us as a burden, but that we're the reason that makes His heart happy and makes Him sing. His sons and daughters are his joy!

2. Jesus wants to share the Father's joy with us

There are those who think of Jesus as someone who accepted suffering with resignation, as someone who served others, but who inside was full of pain as he saw how lost humanity was. They imagine him carrying the great weight of the cross; they visualize a dying man hanging, bleeding and accepting a long and painful death.

It's true that Jesus gave himself up and was slain as the lamb of God so that we can be free from the power of sin, but the purpose of his death wasn't that we should be unhappy, quite the opposite. He did it so that we can find the happiness of salvation!

The Bible affirms that Jesus is our model in everything. His intimate relationship with the Father and his dependence on the Holy Spirit filled his life with joy that radiated to others. His joy didn't depend on the circumstances or the people around him, or on his personal achievements. The source of Jesus' joy was the close relationship he had with his Father.

Jesus wasn't afraid to show his joy. His heart rejoiced with the simple things in life

 Guide your students to complete Activity 3.

People could see in Jesus a fully happy person, and the people who followed him were infected with his joy. Jesus was enthusiastic about life every day he lived on this earth; his life was full of purpose. He wanted to convey to his disciples this fullness of joy that filled and overflowed from his heart.

Before his martyrdom, Jesus prayed once again for his followers. We can see Jesus' concern that his disciples wouldn't lose their joy in the difficult times ahead.

Ask for two volunteers to read John 15:11 and 17:13.

Jesus knew that it's not possible to continue in the Christian life without the Father's joy. A better translation of this passage would be like this: ... "that in them my joy may be perfectly full". Something that characterizes our God is His generosity. He is not mean, holding back His blessings from His sons and daughters. The Holy Spirit fills us with the father's joy, the same joy that filled Jesus. Receiving it and cultivating it depends on us.

God doesn't ignore our sadness and pain. Christians live in a world where there is evil, and that evil that surrounds us often causes us pain and sadness. That's why Jesus has sent us the Holy Spirit who is our Comforter.

Ask students to read John 16:22 in unison. Then ask the class: What is Jesus' promise for his sons and daughters when they go through sadness?

Jesus' promise is that no pain or sadness will be permanent. It may last for a time or until physical death or until Jesus returns and takes us with him to his eternal kingdom. Jesus promised that sadness will be taken away and our hearts will be full of joy, a joy that permeates us and which no one can take away.

We must not forget that God's desire for His children is for us to live an abundant and joyful life. The Bible never condemns us for enjoying the blessings we receive from God. But it does condemn us if we put our hope in material goods, or are ungrateful about what we receive from God and don't share with others (1 Timothy 6:17).

3. How do we cultivate joy?

This joy as a Fruit of the Spirit in the midst of the hardest persecutions was the characteristic that distinguished the first Christians. They lived in a context of religious persecution where many were tortured, enslaved, and/or killed, similar to what many of our fellow Christians face in Arab and communist countries today.

However, Christians in the Western world prefer to avoid anything that can cause pain, escaping problems and seeking the easiest way out. The words of the apostle James may sound strange to us. In James 1:2-3, he says: *"Consider it pure joy, my brothers and sisters, whenever you face trials of many kinds, because you know that the testing of your faith produces perseverance."*

James encourages us to face difficult times with joy, since trials, instead of weakening us, if we face them for what they are, a test of our faith, can strengthen us. But to have that ability to resist difficulties with joy, we must exercise our muscles of joy by constantly practicing the following spiritual disciplines.

Bible reading fills us with joy, as Psalm 119:162 states: *"I rejoice in your promise like one who finds great spoil."* The psalmist testifies that this joy is more precious for those who find it a treasure.

Meeting with other believers to share with each other is another discipline that feeds our joy. In the early church, Christians experienced great joy in hearing the testimonies of the new converts (Acts 15: 3) and the advancement of the church in the mission fields. They were glad to hear news of the apostles and other Christians who were far away serving the Lord. They were glad to meet again after a time of not seeing each other. Christian fellowship brought much joy.

Joy in the early Christians was so firm that neither persecution nor economic deprivation could tear it out of their hearts (2 Corinthians 6:10). In the midst of the trials, they sought the comfort of the Holy Spirit and encouraged each other. They practiced Christian charity, sharing with those who had needs among them and prayed for each other. When we practice the discipline of service, we're filled with joy.

However, **constant prayer** is the most important discipline to always remain cheerful. Paul affirms in 1 Thessalonians 5:16-17: *"Rejoice always, pray continually."* When we talk with God, His joy is transmitted to us and fills us until our heart overflows, heals the wounds of the past and present, moves away sadness, and defeatist thoughts are exchanged for promises full of hope.

In the Christian life, we must learn *the language of praise* and practice it in prayer, in our conversations with other people and also in song.

 Ask your students to complete Activity 4.

The language of complaint, defeat, or despair is not compatible with the joy that accompanies the filling of the Holy Spirit. We cultivate joy when we make our lives an expression of praise to God.

4. Joy can be lost

If we don't cultivate joy, we can lose it. Psalm 51:12a says: *"Restore to me the joy of your salvation…"* This Psalm was written by King David. He had experienced from a young age the happiness of God in his life. In Psalm 23:5, he felt so happy that he exclaimed *"my cup overflows."* David had learned to thank and praise the Lord when everything was going well and also in the midst of problems.

But occupied in the affairs of the kingdom, he drifted away from communion with God and fell into sin, committing adultery with Bathsheba. Then he tried to hide it, sending her husband to the most dangerous position in the battle so that he would die under enemy arrows. David had lost his joy, he no longer prayed, he no longer sang praises, and sadness invaded his heart. He was the richest and most powerful man in Israel; he could do anything he wanted to, but nothing he could do helped him recover his God given joy, which had gone out of his heart. That's why he cried out to God with many tears, feeling sunk in the deepest sadness, feeling that his life no longer made sense if God didn't restore to him the joy of his salvation.

Like David, we experience God's joy for the first time as a result of the experience of salvation. Then through discipleship, we learn to refocus our lives according to what the Bible teaches. Step by step we're transformed in the way we think, feel and act. We stop doing some things because they no longer bring us happiness, and we begin to do others things that fill us with a joy that we had not experienced before. Those who aren't Christians cannot understand.

This is due to the change that occurs in our way of thinking when we rearrange our priorities and desires according to God's will. The things that saddened us before, such as not being able to buy a pair of shoes we wanted, now don't affect us in the same way. But other things which we didn't give much importance to before, such as helping an elderly person carry their bag in the market, now fill us with satisfaction.

In this new life, we soon discovered that we wouldn't exchange any of the external sources of joy, which previously produced in us a temporary state of happiness, for this source of full and inexhaustible joy of God that came to our hearts to stay.

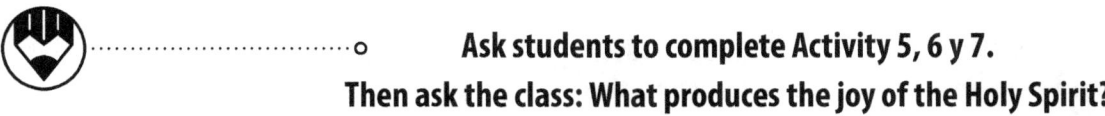

Ask students to complete Activity 5, 6 y 7.
Then ask the class: What produces the joy of the Holy Spirit?

When we ask God to fill us with His Holy Spirit, the joy of the Father floods our hearts. But just like David, we can distance ourselves little by little from communion with God and also lose our joy. So that this doesn't happen to us, we must take care of this treasure, cultivating it through various spiritual disciplines, just as the first Christians did.

Definition of Key Terms

- **Joy:** The word of the New Testament in Greek for the joy that is the Fruit of the Spirit is *charis*. This word is widely used in the Scriptures, especially in the gospels and in the writings of the apostle Paul. It basically means a feeling of inner happiness that manifests itself in words, gestures and acts of joy, and joy.
- **Praise:** Words or songs with which God is praised declaring his glory and his great works in favor of His people, giving thanks for His salvation, His provision and all that He has done, does, and will do for the love of his Church.
- **Charity:** Attitude of solidarity towards people who suffer diverse needs. Charity is giving and providing financial aid, food, clothing, housing, medical care, education and any other type of assistance as the case may be.

Summary

Joy is one of the most obvious characteristics of the Christian life. It's a Fruit of the Spirit that fills our life and that we're responsible for exercising through different spiritual disciplines. When the trials come, being strengthened in the fruit of joy will help us resist and emerge victorious, instead of sinking into an abyss of sadness. We cannot avoid hard times, but we can face them with faith and hope, knowing that no trouble or trial, however strong, can separate us from communion with God, who is the inexhaustible source of joy.

 # Worksheet

ACTIVITY 1
The disease of sadness (depression) can present different symptoms in each person. Identify in the following list if you currently have any of these symptoms in your life.

__ Anhedonia: You don't feel pleasure or satisfaction in almost all of the activities you used to enjoy.

__ Erectile dysfunction in men: Unable to have or maintain an erection to have sex.

__ Inability to reach orgasm: Don't enjoy sex with your spouse as before.

__ Low self-esteem.

__ Feelings of anguish, nervousness.

__ Stopping and not being able to perform your usual tasks.

__ Tiredness or fatigue for no apparent reason.

__ Negative or suicidal thoughts.

__ Changes in mood: You go from euphoria to moments of sadness.

__ Sleep disorder: Don't sleep well, don't rest.

__ Loss of appetite.

__ Lack of concentration.

ACTIVITY 2
What do you do when you feel sad and bored? Point out the activities from the following options that you have chosen at some time to escape sadness and boredom.

__ I go for a run or walk.

__ I practice outdoor sports.

__ I go to the gym.

__ I go on vacation.

__ I drink intoxicating drinks alone or with friends.

__ I take medicine or drugs.

__ I watch TV, movies or internet series.

__ I watch sports.

__ I go to the cinema.

__ I read a book.

__ I surf the web on my phone or computer.

Worksheet - Lesson 4

__ I watch porn.

__ I work until I fall asleep from fatigue.

__ I go shopping.

__ I call a friend or my mother.

__ I sleep.

__ I go out dancing with friends.

__ I listen to music.

__ I eat something really delicious.

__ I cry.

__ I clean the house until it shines.

ACTIVITY 3
In groups of 3 students, investigate in the following passages the occasions that gladdened the heart of God, of Jesus and of God's angels. Order the columns, placing the letter of the column to the right, on the line that corresponds to each verse in the column on the left.

__ Matthew 11:25	A. Eat with new friends.
__ Matthew 19:14	B. Children's receptivity to the Word.
__ Luke 15:5-10	C. Meet with your Church.
__ John 3:29	D. The joy of children.
__ Luke 19:5-10	E. Complete a work commissioned by God.
__ John 17:4	F. A repentant sinner.

Worksheet - Lesson 4

ACTIVITY 4
Indicate in the following list with a letter 'A' those ways of acting and speaking, that convey praise and with a letter 'S', those that convey sadness and hopelessness.

___ Encourage others with promises from God.

___ Use indecent or degrading words.

___ Repeat or forward sexist jokes that degrade people's sexuality.

___ Use negative critical language when talking about others or oneself.

___ Visit a sick person and pray for their healing.

___ Criticize my partner when I am with others.

___ Ventilate intimate affairs of my partner or a friend who were secretly entrusted to me.

___ Making fun of others or giving nicknames pointing out their flaws.

___ Thank God for the daily bread.

___ Receive with love and acceptance the brother who had fallen into sin.

___ Save part of the tithe, in case there's an emergency in the family.

___ Serve in the church in a bad mood, by obligation.

___ Thank my spiritual leaders with small details.

___ Sing praise songs in the morning while I prepare breakfast for my family.

___ Shout at my child every time he leaves his room in disarray.

___ Cry with joy in the midst of the songs of praise.

___ Comfort a young child who got hurt playing.

___ Show a sincere smile when I greet the brothers and sisters in the church.

___ Thank God for the beauty of his creation.

___ Complain to the pastor every Sunday about something I disagree.

___ Insulting a bad driver in the street.

___ Share the gospel and pray for the salvation of a friend.

Worksheet - Lesson 4

ACTIVITY 5
In the following passages of Scripture investigate what produces the fruit of joy in the life of the believer.

Nehemiah 8:10 _____

Psalms 16:9 _____

Psalms 43:4 _____

Isaiah 51:3 _____

Acts 2:26 _____

Romans 15:13 _____

ACTIVITY 6
Answer the following questions:

1. Right now, do you feel sad, discouraged, depressed to the point that you cannot overcome that feeling of sadness that floods you?

2. Do you need to receive healing from emotional wounds from your past, which you have carried for a long time?

3. Have you lost communion with God because of any sins you have committed?

4. Do you fight every day with negative and defeatist thoughts?

5. Are you most of the time in a bad mood and angry? Is your way of talking with others often aggressive?

6. Do you feel envious of another person's happiness because you think it's something you cannot have?

If you have answered yes to any or more of these questions, talk to your teacher or pastor after class for spiritual advice and guidance.

ACTIVITY 7
Make a list of the things you will do this year to cultivate the joy of God in your life. Then in prayer, make a commitment to God and communicate your desire to be filled abundantly with this joy that he has promised his sons and daughters.

My notes

Worksheet - Lesson 4

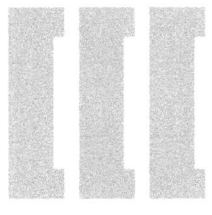

Love that Makes Us Instruments of Peace
Lesson 5

 **Lesson Objectives**

That the students might...

- **Identify** areas of their live where they lack peace.
- **Describe** the beneficial effects of peace as a Fruit of the Spirit.
- **Understand** that peace begins in the mind, directs our emotions and moves our actions.
- **Commit** to being a peacemaker, following the model of Jesus Christ.

 **Visual Aids**

- Newspapers or printed articles from digital newspapers with news of the last month about situations of war, conflict, and violence in your country or area. They can also be statistics on suicides, murders, acts of violence, disagreements between politicians, between companies, between government and unions and others.

Introduction

The third Fruit of the Spirit mentioned in Galatians 5:21 is **peace.** The Greek word that the apostle Paul uses to describe it is *eirene*. Let's look at the meaning of this term as used in the New Testament:

]][Draw the following graph on the board:]][

As we see, the peace we receive from the Spirit cannot be defined merely as the absence of war or armed conflict between nations. It refers to a state of peace that encompasses our entire being, flooding us with a feeling of inner harmony that's reflected in our relationships with the outside world. But for Christians who live in the midst of this turbulent world, this whole idea of peace may seem nothing more than a romantic dream, impossible to realize.

Around us there's a world at war. Beyond the armed conflicts or political differences that exist between some nations, hostile relationships abound at all levels. On an individual level, people barely tolerate each other, get angry easily, break relationships, divorce, make enemies, argue daily, are aggressive and don't know how to resolve their differences and conflicts.

We also live in the midst of new types of wars, such as the war on business, the psychological war, the war on drug cartels, the political war between candidates, the television competitiveness for ratings, the war between trade unions and governments, and the list goes on. It seems that we don't have the option of being out of these wars that surround us on every side.

]][Distribute newspapers or news clippings and ask students to describe what types of wars are being fought in their current context.]][

 Then ask students to complete Activity 1.

In this lesson we're going to ask ourselves: Is it possible to experience this fruit of peace in the middle of a world at war? How can Christians be instruments of peace for those around us?

The Fruit-Filled Life | 55

Bible Study

1. WE ARE CHILDREN OF A GOD OF PEACE

It's difficult to imagine what it's like to live in a world in peace, where each person is at peace with themselves, with God, with others, and with creation. There was complete peace and harmony in the garden of Eden when there was no sin in the human heart.

||| Ask a student to read 2 Corinthians 13:11. |||

The apostle reminds the members of the Corinthian church, who had had a few differences of opinion, that our God is a Father of peace and love. The apostle declares that the only way to remain full of joy and peace is to learn to live in harmony with each other.

Adam and Eve had enjoyed the full Fruit of the Spirit of God in their lives, until they fell into sin. The love they had for each other was replaced by accusations, unity changed to enmity, joy was replaced by sadness, guilt and shame. The snake (Satan) knew that if he broke that bond of trust between the first couple and their Creator, they would be at his mercy.

When the relationships between human beings and God broke down, all other relationships did too. The woman went from being equal, to being an object of desire, subject to man. Men and women were enslaved. Humanity changed its role of caretaker of creation to that of aggressor and destroyer of the natural world.

From that moment on, human history was characterized by acts of cruelty, submission, slavery, killings, wars. The people of Israel were not exempt and, except for short periods of peace, lived almost always in times of war, insecurity and conflict. In the midst of this general state of insecurity, the prophet Isaiah encouraged the people in anticipation of the coming of a Prince of peace.

||| Ask a student to read Isaiah 9:6. |||

God asked the people of Israel to be patient, that God's peace, that lost and so desired peace, was already on its way. The promised peace would come in the form of a person who would be called Jesus of Nazareth. The lamb sent by God wouldn't only end suffering and sickness, the fruit of sin, it would also restore peace at all levels.

2. JESUS CHRIST GIVES US HIS PEACE

On the night of Jesus' birth, the angels proclaimed: *"Glory to God in the highest heaven and on earth peace to those on whom his favor rests."* (Luke 2:14). It wasn't us, but God who took the initiative to make peace with humanity! In that child, God demonstrated His good will. In Jesus, the seed of peace was sown and began to grow in this world.

When studying the books of the New Testament, we have no doubt that Jesus Christ is that seed of peace.

○ **Ask students to complete Activity 2.**

Jesus Christ, the peace of God made man, came into the world. The seed of peace can grow in our hearts today, thanks to the fact that the power of Satan has been defeated on the cross. Isaiah 53:5 says: *"But he was pierced for our transgressions, he was crushed for our iniquities; the punishment that brought us peace was on him, and by his wounds we're healed."*

Satan has no power over our life, unless we give him permission. But if there's any area of our being that has not yet been submitted to Jesus Christ, we won't be able to experience the full peace that God wants to give us.

Ask a student to read Romans 16:20.

In Romans 16:20, Paul affirms that Jesus Christ is the one who has the power to crush Satan and put him under our feet. God anticipated in Genesis 3:15: *"And I will put enmity between you and the woman, and between your offspring and hers; he will crush your head, and you will strike his heel."* This promise was fulfilled in Jesus Christ and is available to us today.

Because of Jesus' sacrifice on the cross, the path was opened so that all relationships can be restored. The reconciliation of people with God in the experience of salvation is the beginning. From there, thanks to the work of the Holy Spirit, the peace of God is poured into the heart of every disciple of Jesus, and all other relationships can be restored.

Ask students to read Colossians 1:19-20 and then look at the graph that's part of Activity 3. Ask the class: Why is restoration of relationships with ourselves, with others and with our Creator so important if we want to live in peace?

Jesus Christ, just before he ascended to heaven, full of authority, gave his disciples his peace.

3. THE HOLY SPIRIT, THE GREAT PEACEMAKER

The greatest gift that the Holy Spirit brings to our lives is peace. It wouldn't be possible for us to have the experience of this full peace without the ministry of the Holy Spirit.

Ask students to read John 14:25-27 in unison. Then ask the class: What things rob Christians of peace today?

Jesus was preparing his disciples for the hard times they would face, not only because their Master was going to be crucified, but because after seeing him again after the resurrection, they would be separated again since he was going to return to heaven to be with his Father. So far, Jesus had been their teacher, leading them in the mission, but also, he kept them focused on the path of peace. When Jesus left, His Spirit assumed these three functions so necessary for the permanence of the disciples and for the health of the early church: He would be their teacher, guiding them in the mission and He would bring them peace. How can we experience the peace that the Spirit wants to give us?

Ask a student to read 1 Thessalonians 5:23.

The only way to experience the full peace of God is to live in holiness. The life of holiness and spiritual peace come together. But for that peace to be complete, it must fill our spirit, soul and body, in other words, our whole being, and reveal itself to the world through our actions.

Ask students to complete Activity 4.

Spiritual peace

The first area of our being that's filled with the peace of God is the spirit. Romans 5:1 states: *"Therefore, since we have been justified through faith, we have peace with God through our Lord Jesus Christ…"*

When the Lord has cleansed our sins and we live a holy and transparent life before Him, our spirit is at peace with God. The peace of the human spirit is only possible when we lay down the weapons we had raised in rebellion against God and surrender to the lordship of Christ, accepting to live under the laws of his kingdom.

Mental peace

Peace of mind is a precious gift for contemporary people. It goes by different names: mood peace, soul peace, inner peace, mental peace. It's described as a state of stillness, of tranquility, of inner calm, of absence of restlessness, anxiety, worry or anguish.

**Ask a student to read Psalm 4:8 and ask the class:
How does the psalmist describe this peace that comes from God?**

The psalmist describes a state of mental peace that helps him achieve a deep and restorative sleep at night. Such deep sleep fills us with energy, and helps us be in good spirits during the day. All the cells of our body regenerate with a night of calm, deep and restful sleep.

To live in peace, we need a peaceful mind. In John 15:25-27, Jesus said that it's the Spirit who keeps fresh the memory of what we learned from the Word, including the good examples we have in Jesus. He also reminds us of the experiences of other people who walked in the faith before us, the teachings we receive from our teachers in the church, and the good advice of our brothers and sisters in the faith.

The Holy Spirit can only do this if we have spent time learning from the Word and if we have filled our minds with valuable teachings for the Christian life. Then when the time comes, the Spirit can bring from our subconscious mind what we need to remember from the Word of God so that we can face every situation that disturbs us.

When the circumstances around us make our spirit and mind restless, instead of trying to find a solution by trying to work it out by ourselves, let's take time to pray and let the Holy Spirit act. If we learn to divert our thinking from the problem to focus on the Word God and pray, asking to be flooded with the peace of God, our mind can be at peace at all times. Even if we don't see the solution, we can rest assured that God will show us the step in a timely manner.

Ask a student to read Philippians 4:7.

This peace that invades our spirit and mind also comes to pacify emotions and will. Our emotions and will depend on our thoughts. If our mind is restless, we'll feel restless and it will affect how we behave. To be at peace with other people, we must first have peaceful thoughts about them.

Peace for the body

When we're a sick, when we lose our health, we usually lose peace too. Disease and deterioration suffered by our physical body is one of the consequences of sin. A disease can be caused by the person who suffers from it, or by the surrounding environment.

There are diseases that are the result of personal sin or bad stewardship of our bodies. We are responsible for what we eat, the exercise we do, the workload we carry, the rest we get, etc. Other conditions are caused by vices and sins that involve the body, such as sexual debauchery, addictions to tobacco, drugs, alcohol, among others. There are also diseases for which we aren't responsible, but that we can acquire by genetic inheritance, by vices of people with whom we live (such as tobacco), by bad stewardship of the creation of our neighbors (such as water, air and soil pollution) and others.

As long as we live in a world contaminated by sin, we won't have perfect healing for our bodies. However, it's also true that the life of holiness brings great benefits to our integral health. This is primarily due to the abandonment of sin.

Ask a student to read John 5:14. Ask the class:
Why does Jesus give this warning to the paralytic?

When Jesus performed miracles of healing, he sent those who had placed their faith in him on their ways, healthy and in peace. In Mark 5:34, Jesus said to the woman whom he healed from the flow of blood, "Daughter, your faith has healed you. Go in peace and be freed from your suffering." This woman had lived for twelve years at war with her own body. When we get sick, our body becomes a battleground between bacteria, viruses, germs, bacilli, microorganisms etc. Healing comes when the Spirit of God defeats these harmful armies.

The woman had also lived full of fear, with pain. For twelve years she was deprived of the affection of her family. Because of the flow of blood, Jewish law considered her impure. That same law prohibited her from going to the temple to seek help from God. Apparently, she was a woman who had had financial resources, but had been left in poverty because doctors had taken all her money with false promises to find a cure for her condition.

The disease had stolen her peace. Jesus not only restored her health, but he sent her to restart her life in complete peace. We don't know what caused her illness, or all the scorn and abuse she had suffered in those long years. But from that time forward, she had to forgive and start a new life in peace with everyone.

 **Ask students to complete Activity 5.**

4. Serving the world as instruments of peace

Jesus taught the disciples to live in peace with each other and also with others. On several occasions, the disciples tried to fix the conflicts in their own way, or in the way of their culture. Let's see some examples.

On one of their trips, the disciples got angry with the inhabitants of Samaria who denied them lodging and food. James and John proposed what they thought was a "fair" retribution for the rude treatment they had received. They asked, *"Lord, do you want us to call fire down from heaven to destroy them?"* (Luke 9:54).

The Fruit-Filled Life

Jesus' reaction was swift. The gospel says that he rebuked them (Luke 9:55). Jesus makes it clear that the advancement of his kingdom will never be through weapons and violence. Peace can never be achieved by violent means. Yes, the kingdom of God is a kingdom of conquest, but we're called to conquer the souls of people through the gospel of grace, love and peace.

Ask a student to read Matthew 20:20-28. Ask the class: What petition did John and James bring to Jesus?

James and John tried to climb positions in the "ecclesiastical hierarchy" using their influence. They came to make a request of Jesus, using their mother as a spokesperson. Imagine the scene ... the three kneeling before Jesus, the mother speaks for them and goes straight to the point. The brothers who always talked were quiet, waiting to see if their plan would work out.

Upon hearing the request, Jesus doesn't rebuke the woman - knowing that she had been used - but speaks to her sons. Jesus' patience with his disciples is admirable, tolerating their greed, their jealousy, their excessive ambition. James and John revealed the darkest intentions of their hearts. They wanted to outdo the other disciples, climb positions, monopolize power and authority over others. Their motives were selfish, carnal. The rest of the disciples were rightly angry with them and, once again, Jesus intervenes to keep the peace between them and teaches them a valuable lesson about a new model of spiritual leadership, the model of servant-hood.

Peace in the world and in the church won't be achieved through leadership that exerts strength, dominance and authoritarianism over people. A leader who uses people as subjects to achieve his ends is not worthy of the kingdom of God. The life of the Christian leader must be one of service, regardless of his or her function. The weapons of such service are tools that cultivate peace; they are arms that extend to serve with education, food, health, housing, affection, comfort, and friendship.

Although James and John learned their lesson, Peter - perhaps the most stubborn of the disciples - was the last to understand that the sons and daughters of God shouldn't practice any form of violence.

Read John 18:9-10.

Having cut off the ear of the High Priest's servant, called Malchus, who had come to arrest Jesus, Peter was stopped by his Master. Jesus restored the wounded ear of that man and Peter finally understood that we must trust God with our life and our destiny, giving ourselves completely into his hands. Years later, he recommends to Christians in 1 Peter 3:10-12: *"For, 'Whoever would love life and see good days must keep their tongue from evil and their lips from deceitful speech. They must turn from evil and do good; they must seek peace and pursue it. For the eyes of the Lord are on the righteous and his ears are attentive to their prayer, but the face of the Lord is against those who do evil."*

The disciples learned that the followers of Jesus have the job of being builders of peace. The popular saying "the end justifies the means" is not valid as a norm of conduct for the sons and daughters of the God of peace. God has not only given us a mission, a purpose for our lives, he has also provided us with the tools we're going to use: the fruit of his Spirit.

Peace is one of our most powerful tools. As a church, we should be that oasis of peace in the middle of a world at war. We are called to be peace builders in our community, serving as mediators and teaching people how to resolve their conflicts.

As we approach the second coming of Christ, our challenge will increase, for there will be less peace in families and in the world (Revelation 6:4). We won't be surround by peace if we don't work hard to create it.

 **Guide your students to complete Activity 6.**

Definition of Key Terms

- **Aromatherapy**: Method of cure of some diseases based on the effects that are produced by the aromas of essential oils of plants on the body. Some of these treatments are used to relieve anxiety, depression, nervousness, stress, physical and mental fatigue and sleep disorders. The oils are used in body massages, in aromatic baths, for infusions and also with aroma diffusers.
- **Contentment:** State of joy, satisfaction, happiness.
- **Mind control:** It's a technique whose purpose is to direct mental activity, dominating thoughts and transforming the way of thinking. It lends itself to the manipulation, brainwashing and coercive pursuit of other people.
- **War:** Refers to a state of hostility that unleashes fighting in battle between individuals, families or peoples.
- **Peace:** In the Old Testament, the Hebrew word *shalom* is used, which means peace, integrity, well-being, health. It's a way to greet visitors that was and is common to the people of Israel. In the New Testament, the Greek word *eirene* describes the harmonic relations between people and nations, friendship, the absence of aggression and order in the state and churches.
- **Yoga:** Philosophical doctrine that practices relaxation techniques, breathing, asceticism and different body postures in order to reach a state of spiritual perfection and peace of mind, through physical and mental control. It's typical of the Hindu religion.

Summary

The peace of the Father, the peace that Jesus left us and with which the Holy Spirit fills us, is perfect, complete and His peace can invade our whole being. The peace of God is poured into our spirit when the Holy Spirit fills our life. From there the Spirit acts in our mind, filling us with peaceful thoughts, which in turn generate peaceful feelings and actions.

Every Christian is called to be a peacemaker in their environment, starting with their family and the church itself.

 **Worksheet**

ACTIVITY 1
Put a check next to the areas of your life in which you're facing conflicts or situations that steal your peace.

Areas where I currently have problems:

__ Acceptance of myself (my body, my character, other)

__ Relationships with one or more people in my family

__ Relations at work / place of study

__ Situation with a friend, boyfriend/girlfriend

__ Financial situation

__ Crime in my country / community

__ Violent neighbors or those that cause problems

Origin of the conflict(s) I currently have:

__ Difference of ideas, interests or opinions

__ Difference of values

__ Impossibility of achieving my plans and goals

__ Clash of character

__ Intolerance, I dislike the person

__ Differences or conflicts in the past

ACTIVITY 2
In groups of 3, search the following Bible passages and answer the questions.

a). Where must the peace of God be rooted before we can take it to others? (Luke 1:79)

_____
_____

b). How did the risen Christ greet the disciples who hid for fear of those who persecuted them? (Luke 24:36, John 20:19, 26.)

_____
_____

Worksheet - Lesson 5

c). Christ came to break down the barriers between nations. He began by uniting Jews and Gentiles in the Church. Mention some of the walls that divide people today. (Ephesians 2:14)

_____

_____

d). In your opinion and according to Colossians 1:20, is it correct to say that the peace treaty between heaven and humanity was signed with the blood of Jesus? Could peace have been achieved in another way?

_____

_____

ACTIVITY 3

ACTIVITY 4
In the following list put a check next to the false paths by which people, in their context, may seek spiritual, mental and emotional peace.

__ Physical exercise

__ Yoga

__ Meditation

__ Relaxing or soothing medicines

__ Listen to music

__ Go on vacation

__ Mental control

__ Aromatherapy

__ Amulets and objects that "radiate" positive energy

__ Cleaning by sorcerers

__ Diet to detoxify the body

__ Do what people want / keep them happy

__ Avoid conflict / Don't say what I think / Lying

Worksheet - Lesson 5

ACTIVITY 5
Below you will find four columns. Each list shows examples of things that cause a lack of peace. Point out those that are present in your life today. Then answer: What is the area of my life that needs to be filled with the full peace of God?

Spiritual	Mental	Emotional	Physical
sin	doubting God	sadness	verbal violence
disobedience	worry	cowardice	addictions
fear of death	negativity	anxiety	anorexia/bulimia
guilt	fear	nervousness	adultery
	distrust	anger	debauchery
	division	fanaticism	depression
	prejudices	impatience	insomnia
	intolerance	low self-esteem	exhaustion
	greed	suicidal thoughts	sexual immorality
	bad thoughts		

ACTIVITY 6
Re-write the following prayer of St. Francis of Assisi in your own words, adapt it to your life today. Then, pray to the Lord, using the words you have chosen.

Lord make me an instrument of your peace
Where there is hatred let me sow love
Where there is injury, pardon
Where there is doubt, faith
Where there is despair, hope
Where there is darkness, light
And where there is sadness, joy

O divine master grant that I may
Not so much seek to be consoled as to console
To be understood as to understand
To be loved as to love
For it's in giving that we receive
It's in pardoning that we're pardoned
And it's in dying that we're born to eternal life.
Amen

Worksheet - Lesson 5

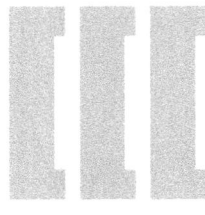

Love that Produces Unlimited Patience
Lesson 6

 **Lesson Objectives**

That the students might...

- **Recognize** the need to cultivate the fruit of patience in their lives.
- **Identify** those situations in which they easily lose patience.
- **Become** acquainted with examples of patience in the Bible.
- **Identify** disciplines to develop patience in their lives.

 **Visual Aids**

Choose one of the following options to arouse interest at the beginning of the class:
- A board game that requires a lot of patience, for example: Jenga, a magic cube, jigsaw puzzles, pick-up-sticks or others.
- A box of paper clips and link them in a long chain.
- Untangle wool/yarn that's all tangled up.
- Place Dominoes in a vertical row, next to each other.
- Pieces of fabric to embroider by hand.

Introduction

Start the class with the activity you have prepared. Give them enough time for everyone to participate. At the end encourage discussion with these questions: How are you getting on? Do you think that if we didn't have patience we would be able to do this activity? Why are these games important for children? What was the most frustrating part of participating in this activity?

Patience is the fruit that follows love, joy and peace in Paul's list in Galatians 5:22-23. In the passage of 1 Corinthians 13:4, the apostle affirms that *"love is patient,"* and later in verse 7, he also says that love *"always hopes"*. Patience is an art that all Christians need to cultivate.

Ask students to complete Activity 1. Then ask the class: What are some daily circumstances of life that make you lose patience? Do you think that people in your context consider patience a virtue or a weakness?

The Greek word that translates "patience" in the New Testament is the noun *makrothumia*. In the Greco-Roman culture which surrounded the New Testament church, patience wasn't considered a virtue. So, we can affirm that patience came to be considered a virtue as a result of the gospel message and the practice of the life of holiness.

Both the noun *makrothumia*, and its verbal form *makrothumein*, describe a virtue and an attitude. We can learn about this virtue from the good examples we find in the Bible, in Church history, and through the testimonies of our brothers and sisters in our churches. But, as we'll study below, our main model of patience is God Himself.

Bible Study

1. THE PATIENCE OF GOD

Patience is one of the great characteristics of God's love. On different occasions in history, people have pushed the Creator's patience to the limit. Upon returning from captivity in Babylon and Persia, the Levites sang a psalm thanking God for his patience, which is recorded in the book of Nehemiah.

Ask a student to read Nehemiah 9:29-31. Then ask the class: What did the Israelites do that tried God's patience?

For many years, the people of Israel abused God's patience. They knew they were guilty. Although they received the warnings of the prophets about the danger they were exposing themselves to by causing the Lord's wrath, they persisted in their lives of sin. Many Israelites thought that the words of the prophets would never be fulfilled. They had become accustomed to sinning every day. They were confident that their "little disobediences" went unnoticed by God and, in fact, many of them died without seeing God's judgment materialize. However in its time, God's judgment came upon the nation and it was their children and grandchildren who suffered exile.

Something happened that's hard for us to understand. Far from abandoning His people, God's loving patience was manifested again. At last, they were willing to learn to live in holiness, and God taught them once again to live in obedience. This rebellious people, to whom God showed so much patience, was a key instrument in God's restorative mission for humanity. God's patience with Israel bore its fruit and it's through Jesus Christ that now all the peoples of the earth can know the God of love and compassion.

[[[Ask a student to read 2 Peter 3:8-9.]]]

Then ask the class to complete Activity 2.

In Jesus' life we can see how the fruit of patience was present. Jesus learned to be patient with his Father. He was patient with the people who came to him for help, many of whom showed no consideration of his human frailty or his need to rest or eat. He showed patience with the disciples who had immature and selfish attitudes. He was patient with his mother and his brothers who often didn't understand the demands of his call and his mission (Matthew 3: 31-34). He even showed patience with those who tortured him, enduring suffering.

2. EXAMPLES OF PATIENCE

Noah is one of the greatest examples of patience. Before the flood, people lived for many years, in some cases reaching more than 900 years of age. It's hard to imagine a birthday cake with 900 candles, right?

Ask students to complete Activity 3.

Noah learned to be patient because he trusted that God would keep His promises. How many of us would have had the perseverance to wait for a hundred years? It would take us a lifetime, but we often have trouble just waiting for a year, five years or even ten years.

Noah didn't sit down to wait, but worked hard with his eyes set on the goal God had given him. This is one of the characteristics of Noah's type of patience, patience that is the Fruit of the Spirit. This patience is one that trusts and hopes, but at the same time works and acts. God formed a team with Noah and his family. Each one had to fulfill his part of the plan so that the human race and the animals had the opportunity to survive.

Finally, Noah and his family saw God's promise fulfilled. However, it's important to note that there are promises that we probably won't see fulfilled during our time here on earth.

In 2 Peter 3:8-9, the apostle Peter teaches that we shouldn't judge God's time according to our perspective. Today we live life in an accelerated way; we're people of the 'fast food culture', of flying across the world in a few hours, of instant communications. We have little patience for waiting and little tolerance for lateness. From our rushed pace, we may think that God is slow, but this is not so. His way of measuring time is different from ours, and His patience is infinitely greater than ours.

The fact that God waits patiently to fulfill His promise of the second coming of Christ is not a sign of weakness or indecision to act. This delay, rather, is evidence of His love and mercy towards all the families of the earth, in order to give them the opportunity to be saved (Matthew 13: 24-29). We have a God willing to adjust His agenda for the love of the lost! While we wait for this event that will begin a new stage in the history of salvation, like Noah, we must remain engaged in the mission that God has entrusted to us.

Abraham is another biblical example of patience. God called him out of his land when he was 75 years old and he walked with God until he was 175 years old. In Genesis 15:1-7 God made a covenant with Abraham…

[[[Ask a student to read Genesis 15:1-7.]]]

God promised the land of Canaan to Abraham. He also promised him that he would be the Father of a great nation, but the problem was that Abraham and his elderly wife and had no children. Such a promise was hard to accept. In those days, there were no fertility clinics or ways to know if it was possible that at some point Sara would get pregnant. When Abraham and Sara looked at the odds with the knowledge they had at that time, all the logical conclusions led them to affirm that this was an impossible promise to fulfill.

Imagine that our home is in a desert where we have never seen a drop of rain fall in our lives, and God told us that this dry and sterile place was going to become a green valley, full of fruit, in which there will never more be a shortage of water. Would it be easy for us to believe that this could really happen?

In Hebrews 6:15, it says: *"And so after waiting patiently, Abraham received what was promised."* Against all human logic and all scientific probability, Abraham waited and waited. Years later, when Abraham was 100 years old and Sara about 90, Isaac was born. Abraham's story teaches us that we need to be patient to see divine blessings. The waiting time was worth it.

The last example we have selected for this lesson is Job. The book of Job is a masterpiece of universal literature and is probably the oldest book in the entire Bible. It's difficult for most people to put themselves in Job's shoes and understand the depth of the tragedies that came one day after another in his life.

In modern terms, we could say that Job was a successful man, someone who had realized all his dreams. Thanks to his work and diligence, he had a fruitful enterprise, money in the bank, a beautiful wife, children, property, good health and above all, he felt satisfied because he had cultivated a beautiful relationship with God. Job didn't owe anything to anyone, not even to his God.

[[[Ask a student to read Job 1:1-3.]]]

Job was a man with a pure and clean heart before God. His plan was to reach old age in happiness, enjoying his family, his grandchildren and the fruit of his work. But suddenly his life changed completely.

The Fruit-Filled Life

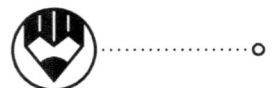 **Ask students to complete Activity 4 and then make a list on the board of the hardships that suddenly came into Job's life.**

Imagine for a moment how Job felt. Psychologists or psychiatrists would rightly say that he was going through trauma, and that he had sunk into depression. What would we do in that situation? Would we complain? Would we blame God or others? Would we blame ourselves?

Possibly we would wait as he did for a helping hand to come to comfort us and give us some hope. Job's four friends arrived, but instead of encouraging him, their words plunged him even deeper into despair. Paraphrasing his friends, it went something like this: "Think well Job, because you have obviously done something very bad for God to punish you in this way." They took Job to the limit of his resistance, to the point that he finally asked them not to talk anymore: *"You, however, smear me with lies; you are worthless physicians, all of you! If only you would be altogether silent! For you, that would be wisdom"* (Job 13:4-5).

Despite the great pain of his losses, Job knew that it wasn't God who was punishing him. He had enough sanity to reject the unhealthy advice of his four friends, who instead of healing his wounds, rubbed salt in them with their words of criticism and accusation. When a faithful Christian goes through times of trials, what they need is the love and comfort of their leaders and brothers and sisters in the faith. Job waited patiently for the storm to pass, and God rewarded him by restoring his life. He got well, regained his business, formed a new family, and lived 40 more years enjoying a blissful old age (Job 42:12).

Throughout this recovery process, Job never doubted that God was with him. Despite the advice of those around him, he never distrusted God's love for him and never stopped worshiping and serving him. Job waited for God, remained faithful in hard times, and was finally rewarded.

3. PATIENCE IN DAILY LIFE

The Greek word *makrothumia*, used in Galatians 5:22, points to another characteristic of this Fruit of the Spirit; it refers to the ability to tolerate for a long-time difficult circumstances that come into our lives, such as problems, diseases, offenses, wounds, provocations made by other people, etc.

Patience is especially observable in Christian behavior in the way we handle our interpersonal relationships. Patience acts with perseverance and constancy: they are an inseparable trio.

||| Draw the following graph on the board. |||

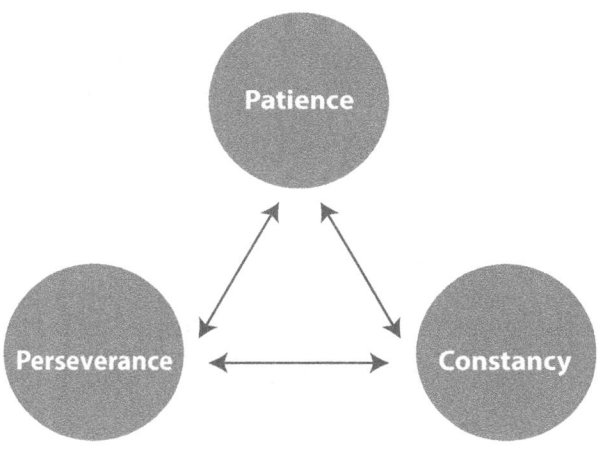

 **Ask students to complete Activity 5.**

It's impossible to live the Christian life faithfully without patience. Some are confused to think that patience is synonymous with sitting and waiting, or not intervening when an act of injustice occurs before our eyes, or not reacting when someone attacks us. But as we saw in Noah's example, the patience of the Christian must be active, dynamic.

First, we must be patient with ourselves and give ourselves the space we need to develop healthily in all areas of life. Today, Christians are subject to many pressures. The accelerated pace of life that many of us lead pushes us to the limit. It's important that we examine our goals and the deadlines we set for achieving them. The goals must be realistic and consistent with our individual possibilities. In Ecclesiastes 3:1, it says: *"There is a time for everything, and a season for every activity under the heavens."*

We aren't mere machines. We're created beings with a supreme purpose - having communion with God, getting to know our Creator deeply, and learning from Him. But most Christians today don't have time to pray, to do Bible-study, or even to cultivate relationships with their family and with members of their church. The activities that should be the most important in our lives have become the ones we neglect the most. We get carried away by the world's priorities, its goals, by the eagerness to succeed, and so on, without realizing that we're hurting ourselves and we're missing the best of life. We need to ask God to teach us to see our life with His eyes and to give us wisdom to design our life project so that it will be in every way pleasing to Him.

Secondly, patience should help us serve others better. Christian leaders who put too much pressure on people on their teams are usually the ones who demand too much of themselves. Learning to respect our limits will help us to be patient and respect the limits of others. Impatience with ourselves drives us to be less tolerant of others. It will also lead to frustration and exhaustion. There are many Christian leaders who fail in their ministries because they put pressure on themselves and on their teams beyond their limits.

In the New Testament, patience is an essential characteristic for exercising spiritual leadership and leading a local congregation (2 Corinthians 6:6, 1 Timothy 1:16, 2 Timothy 3:10). It's also a quality that everyone who preaches the Word must have (Titus 2:2) since the teaching of the Bible must be delivered with love and not with anger.

Patience is then indispensable for the exercise of the ministry to which we have been called and for our fellowship among Christians. The best way to develop this fruit in our lives is to work with others. Something as simple as singing together or reading the Bible in unison requires patience. When we're patient with our fellow Christians, we'll show them how much we love them.

Ask students to complete Activity 6.

Thirdly, patience as a Fruit of the Spirit must be present in all the circumstances of our life. All people act patiently in some situations. Mothers are patient with their children, teachers are patient with their pupils, etc. But Christian patience must be visible in every situation we face and in all our dealing with other people. There are Christians who are patient with church people, but very intolerant of their own family. Others have patience with themselves, or with their friends, but are impatient with others.

The situations of conflict with other people, especially with those who attack us or grieve us, challenge our patience. When someone attacks us or hits us, our natural reaction is to be aggressive back. We desire for revenge! Maybe folks around us will applaud us for hitting back, but the love of God dwelling in our hearts doesn't allow us to respond in this way. God's patience is our model. Even if we have the opportunity to avenge ourselves, our duty is to decide not to.

Guide your students to complete Activity 7.

We cannot choose when and with whom to be patient or not. Our challenge then is to be patient in every situation. We are responsible for being patient with our neighbors just as God has been with us.

The Fruit-Filled Life | 71

Definition of Key Terms

- **Attitude:** Disposition of mind that's demonstrated in the way we think, react to situations and act. It can also be observed in our tone of voice, body posture, gestures, and other forms of nonverbal expression.
- **Trials:** Persevere or persist in a goal.
- **Hope:** For Christians, hope means trusting and waiting for what God has promised. Our hope is different from worldly expectations because it doesn't focus on temporary things, but on the eternal, immortal and almighty God. Faith and hope walk together, they grow and strengthen during the life of the Lord's disciples (Hebrews 11:1).
- **Perseverance:** In the New Testament, perseverance describes the persistence of Christians in their walk with Christ until the end of their lives (Hebrews 12:1). Maintaining a close relationship with God every day is the responsibility of every believer, because if they neglect this relationship with God, they can fall back into the life of sin and reject their salvation (1 Corinthians 9:27).
- **Tolerance:** Respect for the ideas, beliefs or practices of others when they are different or contrary to our own. Patience and understanding towards the people who are learning, the weak, the undisciplined, etc.
- **Virtue:** Willingness to think and act according to certain ideals such as love, justice, goodness, etc.

Summary

Patience is one of the virtues of divine love that God gives us with the Fruit of the Spirit. Patient love is a love that's evident in the Christian life in dealing with other people, in our relationship with God, and in our behavior in the face of life's problems and adverse circumstances.

Patience is a fruit, which like the others, we're responsible for cultivating. We learn patience from the example of others and from our own experience by trusting in God's promises and relating to other people. Patient love is essential for our service to God and others.

We need patience, faith and hope so as not to lose the goal of the Christian life, and arrive faithfully when we meet our Lord.

 **Worksheet**

ACTIVITY 1
Answer each questions by writing 'Yes' or 'No' on the line:

___ Have you been impatient or intolerant of anyone recently?

___ When you're in a line waiting for a turn to be helped, do you feel upset and uncomfortable?

___ If a friend tells you a "long" story, do you look at the clock or interrupt them and apologize?

___ Do you get angry if food is not served quickly in a restaurant?

___ When you drive, do you honk if the vehicle ahead of you is driving slower than you are?

___ When the neighbors of your apartment have a party, does the noise bother you enough that you complain in anger?

ACTIVITY 2
Read the passage from 2 Peter 3:8-9 again and then respond according to your personal experience. In what areas have you been resistant to obeying or submitting to God's will in the past? How patient has God been with you?

_____

_____

_____

ACTIVITY 3
In groups of three to four, investigate the following passages and find some details of the life of Noah and his family.

How old was Noah when he became a father? What were his children's names? (Genesis 5:32)
_____

What did people do to exhaust God's patience? (Genesis 6:5-7)
_____

How many years did Noah persevere in building the ark? (Genesis 5:32; 7:6)
_____

How many weeks did Noah wait for the flood to end? (Genesis 7:17-24)
_____

How many years did Noah live? (Genesis 9:28-29)
_____

Worksheet - Lesson 6

ACTIVITY 4
In groups of two, make a list of all the hardships that came into Job's life according to Job 1:6 to 2:10.

_____
_____
_____
_____
_____
_____
_____
_____
_____

ACTIVITY 5
Put the following columns in order by placing the letter of the first column in front of the statement in the second column as appropriate. What is the verse that corresponds to each statement?

	Verse		Affirmation
A	Hebrews 6:12		In the midst of suffering we should rejoice in hope and persevere in prayer.
B	Romans 12:12		Prayer helps us constantly demonstrate our gratitude to the Lord.
C	Romans 8:25		While we wait for the fulfillment of God's promises, we must continue to work and serve people with love.
D	Colossians 4:2		Our constancy is demonstrated when we patiently wait for what we still cannot see.

ACTIVITY 6
Below you will find a list of things we do in the church to help and serve others. Check those for which you still need more patience

__ Babies who cry during the service.

__ Listen to a person who speaks confusingly or with a very soft tone.

__ Answer questions from new people in the church.

__ Help the elderly get to their seats or get to their car.

Worksheet - Lesson 6

__ Sing in the choir with people who find it hard to learn the tunes and melodies.

__ Clean up juice that the children have spilled.

__ A sermon that lasts a long time.

__ Members who are late for the committee meeting.

__ Parents who don't bring their children to activities on time.

__ Members who forget to bring what they promised.

__ The lazy people.

__ The spiritually weak or discouraged.

ACTIVITY 7
Below is a series of situations in which the Bible teaches us to act patiently. In the middle column, underline the words that describe your current reaction, and then in the right column, underline the practices you need to develop.

Situation	My current reaction	Practices I need to develop
Problems or situations that are difficult to resolve	Makes me feel desperate, fills me with anxiety, paralyzes me, I blame others, evade my responsibilities.	Pray for the Lord's help. Look for help. Work to solve the problem. Think with hope. (Romans 5:3-5)
Interpersonal Differences	I criticize, argue, respond with pride, evade conflict, give up, end the relationship, take revenge, refuse to say hello or talk to that person.	Pray for wisdom and love from the Lord. Seek advice. Confront with love. Forgive. Ask for forgiveness if I have offended someone.
Cultural Differences	I criticize, belittle, turn away, point out the negative, join a separate group, change churches.	Pray for love and understanding. Try to understand, cultivate relationships, look for the positive.
Conflict with authority	I criticize, participate in events out of protest, paint graffiti, try to discredit the person on social media.	Pray for tolerance and love to forgive. Speak lovingly to help them see their mistake. Convince them to change the situation. Return good for bad.
Political, economic, social crisis in the country	I don't get involved, I complain, promote violence, insult those responsible, take advantage of the situation.	Pray for wisdom for the government. Help those who are affected. Be part of the solution. Be an instrument of peace and understanding. (Isaiah 28:16)

Worksheet - Lesson 6

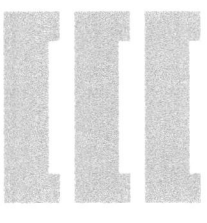

Love Shown in Solidarity to Others
Lesson 7

 **Lesson Objectives**

That the students might...

- **Understand** that true worshipers practice justice and love for the needy.
- **Commit** to building a fairer and more supportive society.
- **Leave** the individualistic and consumerist lifestyle behind them.
- **Adopt** the merciful love of God as a way of life.

 **Visual Aids**

- Three sheets of paper on which you will write a secret mission for three of your students. These papers will be folded or placed in envelopes and placed on a table before students arrive to the class. Write on the outside of each one: "Secret Mission". Write one of these activities on each of the sheets:

    a. In the first 10 minutes of the class, take something from some of your classmates without asking permission and don't give it back to them even if they insist.

    b. In the first 5 minutes of the class, annoy one or two classmates, for example: pull their hair, tickle them, give them a gentle kick, and don't apologize.

    c. In the first 10 minutes of the class, criticize several classmates, for example: criticize their clothes, hairstyle, face, say that you're angry with them because the other day they didn't greet you, etc. Don't apologize at any time for your bad attitude.

- Small bags, some with candies, others with chocolates and others with popcorn. Have enough bags for all of your students. In each bag place an odd number of goodies, for example 5, 7 or 9 pieces.

76 *The Fruit-Filled Life*

Introduction

[[[Choose three students to take the envelopes and keep them secret. Tell them that no one should know the content of their mission, until the time, during class, in which the teacher indicates. Continue with the class normally, ignore interruptions, if someone is offended and reacts strongly, ask students if they have any problems to please resolve it after class.]]]

The fifth characteristic of the Fruit of the Spirit mentioned in Paul's list in Galatians 5:22 is loving-kindness. Because of the similarity between the Greek word *chrettes*, loving-kindness, and *christos*, Christ, people in the first century called Christians the *christens*, that is, "the kind people".

[[[Ask the class: If we were to do a survey today of the people in the community, asking: 'From 1 to 10 (1 being the lowest and 10 the highest), how friendly is our church? How do the people of our church react to their neighbors?' What score do they think they would give us?]]]

The dictionary mentions as synonyms for "kindness": gentleness, affability, urbanity, benevolence and courtesy. As synonyms for the adjective "kind" we find: attentive, affectionate, cordial, accommodating and affectionate. Kindness is so rare in today's society that any selfless act of love for one's neighbor shines like light in the dark. But, we have become accustomed to acts of discourtesy and dealing with inconsiderate and rude people everywhere.

 Ask students to complete Activity 1.
Then ask them, how kind are we as a society? Do we value friendly people in our context? How would our community change if we began to treat each other kindly?

Bible Study

1. LOVING-KINDNESS - A QUALITY OF A HOLY LIFE

In the Bible, kindness and deep love of God are inseparable. This demonstration of love is described in the Old Testament with the Hebrew word *jesed*, which is translated as loving-kindness, mercy, generosity. Loving-kindness towards our neighbor is one of the requirements of the holy life that God demands of His people.

[[[Ask a student to read Micah 6:6-8.]]]

The Fruit-Filled Life

Like other prophets, God called Micah to be His spokesman in a time of great political and social problems. Risking his life, Micah raised his voice to defend the peasants whom the centralized government in Jerusalem had stripped of their lands and plunged into poverty. In their time, unfair practices had been legitimized and instead of defending the victims, the judges supported the perpetrators.

In the previous verses of chapter 6, God repeatedly calls them "my people," reminding them of their origin and history of walking together with Him. Israel had lost her memory. Their actions didn't reflect their true identity as God's holy people. They had forgotten their call, their unique mission among all the peoples of the earth.

In verses 6 and 7, Micah describes the arrogance with which the corrupt leaders of the people approached God. By using hypocrisy, they tried to negotiate with God; they tried to bribe Him with gifts and haggle with Him for His blessings. Since they were corrupt, they bribed each other, and they thought that they could also bribe God. They were even willing to offer their children as sacrifices, using that as a currency to twist God's arm!

In that society, everything and everyone had a price. Relationships between people were motivated by interest. No favor was given without exchanging something. They had forgotten that they were sons and daughters of the God who give everything for love. Surprised that God refused to exchange favors with them, they asked the prophet proudly how they should present themselves before God to worship him.

God answers them, although it wasn't the answer they expected. In verse 8, the Lord says that there are three things that his people demand: "But God has already told you what you can do best and what you expect from Him. It's very simple: God wants you to be fair to each other, to be kind to the weakest, and to worship him as your only God."

God says that to be true worshipers, we must make some changes in our lives. From the rest of the Bible we know that to present ourselves before God, we must lead a holy life. Many times we get confused by thinking that God measures our holiness only in the dimension of our relationship with Him. We are wrong if we believe that to be holy means only attending church, giving our offerings and tithes, praying and reading the Bible.

▐▐▐ Draw the following graph on the board. ▌▌▌

The order in which God's demands appear in this verse of Micah 6:8 is important. Let's look:

The Fruit-Filled Life

2. Practice justice

The idea of justice that the Old Testament prophets had is different from ours. It's not an idea or a concept, something that we can discuss or write books about. Here we aren't talking about a court where we have to defend ourselves or claim that the culprits receive the punishment established by law.

Amos 5:24 says, *"But let justice roll on like a river, righteousness like a never-failing stream!"* The justice of which the prophets speak is practiced in relationships between people. It's not enough to have a clear concept of what is fair, but to practice justice in everything we do in our dealings with all people.

In the time of the prophets, God raised His voice to especially defend the weak and defenseless people who were being oppressed.

||| Ask two students to read Isaiah 10:1-2 and 1:17. |||

Through Isaiah, God calls His people to act in defense of those who don't have any power, those who are invisible in societies, the most unprotected, those who don't have the basic conditions to lead a dignified life. Those who have lost hope and who, unless God's people extend a hand to help them out of their situation, won't be able to access a better future. The situation of invisible people of the time of the prophets is the same today: the destitute, the street children, those who live in extreme poverty, those who have been stripped of their property by usurping actions of the powerful, those exploited at work, the heads of household and their children, orphans, foreigners, and the elderly.

Christian churches often have some kind of compassionate ministry such as love baskets with the week's groceries, donations of clothes, or medicines. There are also construction and repair projects for homes, employment exchanges, medical clinics and others, which contribute to solving the need of a family or community. Thank God for the churches that are salt and light through their practice of kindness in their communities!

However, God expects more from us. His plan is to use us as instruments to spill out His justice as a torrent of living water! Imagine a river that grows with the rain, overflowing and sweeping everything in its path. Well, God has given us the mission of eradicating injustice and corrupt systems that permeate our communities, our provinces, and our countries. Today is the time to get up, the Lord tells us, consecrating our professions and also encouraging our young people to train in careers that allow them to make a difference in our societies. It's time for the justice of the kingdom of God to advance on earth. For this we need to leave our comfort zone and use our resources to bring hope to our peoples.

 **Ask the class to complete Activity 2.**

3. Be kind to others

The Hebrew word *jesed* is translated in some versions of the Bible as kindness, goodness, constant love, mercy, faithfulness and devotion. This is one of the most important words of the ethical and theological vocabulary of the Old Testament. The New Testament uses the Greek term *chestotes*, which means gentle, affectionate, of good manners, and being respectful of others. Both terms describe an endearing affection, not a superficial act, but a love that springs from our hearts. This is the kind of love that God has for his people. It's a strong, constant and graceful love, and we're sent out to reveal it to the world.

> **Distribute the bags among all the students. Explain that they can eat the content but only when they have first given most of it to a fellow student. Notice how they relate while doing the activity. See if students who had the task of disturbing others receive gifts, or if they were given gifts because people felt obliged. Encourage the conversation with questions like these: Who was the first person you thought of to give away your sweets to? With which people is it harder to share? How did it feel to have to give the most? How did it feel to receive the most? Those who were discourteous ... Did they feel they deserved the gift? Were there any who exchanged gifts? Did you feel you had the obligation to return the favor? Some gave sweets to others and received nothing? How did that feel? At the end of the discussion, reveal the secret tasks contained in the envelopes.**

Since we see that we aren't used to practicing this selfless love, let's look at some of the characteristics of this kind love that God expects us to practice.

Sincere Love

Doing something for the simple act of fulfilling a task or looking good, or flattering someone, is not genuine kindness. Every act of flattery, either to God or to a person is a farce, a lie. Perhaps we can deceive a person, but we cannot deceive God who knows the intentions of the heart.

> **Ask a student to read Job 32:22 and ask the class: What does God think of flatterers?**

God doesn't support hypocrisy. Flattery is a simulation, a feigned act, a hoax that hides our true intentions. The same goes for bribes, which are a demonstration of exaggerated and even cloying love, which usually seeks to soften the will of the other person to get something they want.

We must be careful when we're approached by people with false kindness, so as not to fall into the traps of flattery which awaken our vanity. Thieves and scammers use these deceptive tactics to gain people's trust.

Genuine kindness has no limitations; there are no minimum requirements when it comes to obeying God's commandments. Kindness focuses on building strong and lasting relationships. It doesn't simply seek to comply with a legal requirement, such as a marriage certificate, but aims to build healthy and strong relationships.

A Constant and Faithful Love

Constant and faithful love is uncommon in contemporary society, where there's a lot of so-called love but without commitment. There's a tendency to relate to God as we have learned to relate to other people. What is our love for God like? Is it a love that's committed? Is it constant and faithful? Do we practice it at all times and in all situations? Can it be seen in our commitment to God's mission? How faithful and constant are we in living according to the principles and values of the kingdom of God? What is the love we practice in the family of faith like?

One of the problems we see in the church today is that often, shallow relationships are built up between members. Today it's quite common for people to decide to change churches and forget their former brothers and sisters. This is a kind of superficial love which seems to cool down over time, that doesn't lead to deep friendships. The early church was known because they loved each other.

> **⦚ Ask a student to read 1 Thessalonians 2:8 and ask the class:
> How does Paul describe his love for the church in Thessalonica? ⦚**

Paul displays here an endearing love for His sheep; He loved them so much that He invested His own life into them. Loving-kindness builds relationships that last through time. As we grow as disciples of Christ, we must learn this new and "revolutionary" way of loving.

Loving-kindness Inspires Confidence

God is faithful in showing us His love which led the psalmist to exclaim: *"may your love and faithfulness always protect me"* (Psalm 40:11b).

> **⦚ Ask a student to read Hebrews 4:16. ⦚**

Because God has been kind to his people and with us in the past, we're confident in seeking him when we're in need. In the same way, Christians should cultivate people's trust in us so that in case of need, they won't hesitate to come to us for help.

This trust must be mutual. Perhaps we meet people whom nobody trusts because of their past or current condition. Even people who don't trust themselves or their potential can change their lives with Jesus. That's why the cultivation of trust is so important. The acts of loving kindness are used mightily by the Holy Spirit, who moves the hearts, who awakens the sleeping minds, who opens the eyes of the spiritual blind, and helps the emotionally paralyzed to walk. And God makes us part of these miracles!

Kindness to Those in Need

Loving kindness shouldn't be limited to our blood family or church members. God knows that we easily forget those who are outside the circle of our relationships, those who are also our neighbors. That's why the Lord includes a long list of people in need in the Prophets' messages and in the commandments of the law. But although this list is immense, it shouldn't be a limitation for our actions since God's merciful love extends to encompass every creature.

We could say that our rule of life should be to do good whenever we can and to all we can. In our current societies, there's no lack of opportunities to be supportive because wherever we look, there are people in need. There's a need for work, health, love, education, housing, friendship, and much more. People in need are found in all strata of society, even in families that have a medium or high economic level.

It's also true that we cannot satisfy all the shortcomings of the people around us, but if we're willing, we can always do something to help a person or a family.

> **⦚ Ask the class: What kind of emotional or spiritual needs do
> the people in our community have? What could we do, as unified
> members of the community, to satisfy any of them? ⦚**

The Fruit-Filled Life

Kindness describes a heart that's generous, that does more than is expected, more than what the average person would be willing to do for another. It's this deep love of God which moved him to surrender his Son to free us from the despair and slavery of sin. God is our model of unified love.

Perhaps we consider ourselves a unified people because we perform an act of service from time to time, for example when we're contribute to the ministries of the church, or when there's a national catastrophe or a tragedy in the community. But these actions, although good, aren't enough. The work of restoration that God wishes to do in people's lives is integral, encompassing the totality of being. It doesn't focus only on satisfying a temporary need. God wants to give you a new future, full of life, of hope! Such a work requires a deep commitment from his sons and daughters.

The discipleship of Jesus transformed the lives of his disciples because he was different from the teachers of his time. The loving kindness of God dwelling in our hearts should move us to invest our lives in others, building strong relationships of brotherhood and friendship.

 **Ask students to complete Activity 3.**

4. Worship the only God

Being a genuine worshiper has nothing to do with others knowing me as a "Christian," or being a member of such and such a church, or belonging to this or that Christian family. It's not about my position or function within the church structure or my service in a ministry, or being a student in a seminary. According to Micah 3:8, we see that the practice of justice and kindness in our interpersonal relationships is the only thing that makes us acceptable in the presence of God. These two practices are the characteristics of the true Christian.

The institutionalization of the church and the construction of sanctuaries, to some extent, have separated us from the world and separated us from our real battlefield. As a result, often what we're doing in our ministries produces little change in the society around us. Every day there's more violence, corruption, malnutrition, social inequality, sexually transmitted diseases, teenage pregnancies, suicides, and abandoned elderly. It seems that the "god" of this world is more powerful than the God that Christians worship.

Ask the class: What can we as a church do differently to eradicate the evils that enslave the people of our community?

That's why Jesus sent us to "go" in the Great Commission (Matthew 28: 16-20), not only as spokespersons for the gospel message, but as innovators of a new society under the values of the kingdom of God, through transforming discipleship that teaches us to live according to Jesus' model.

Knowing our tendency to keep our blessings to ourselves and forget the needs of others, God insists that we get involved in His work of redemption. That is, those of us who belong to God have to be players on his team; we have to embrace His goals; we have to commit to His mission with all that we are and with all that we have.

The lifestyle of the true worshiper is not compatible with an individualistic and materialistic way of living life. These are chains that keep Christians in slavery; they are tricks of Satan to entertain the people of God and separate them from their true mission in this world. When we borrow with credit cards and acquire loans to buy items or goods that aren't really essential, we become slaves of the banks and things become the idols for which we live and work. Let's not forget that Jesus Christ died to free us from all the bonds that enslave us. No kind of oppression is acceptable to our Creator.

 Ask students to complete Activity 4 y 5.

God identifies as true worshipers those who walk every day in the mission with Him. Jesus is our best example; he humbly served the rejected, marginalized and helpless people who cried in the cities. He saw that through lack of good spiritual leadership, these people were disorientated and suffering.

We need to put aside pride and learn to walk in humility, adopting the servant lifestyle. We need to remember that one day, we were also needy, and it was God who hugged us with His loving-kindness. It's God who transformed our life, putting us today in a position where we can help others.

It's thanks to the Fruit of the Spirit that we can practice this merciful and kind love that God has poured into our hearts. Let's make the decision today to let ourselves be used as instruments of God's loving-kindness. Let's work to bring justice and love to the helpless and needy. Let's abandon the individualistic and indifferent posture. Let's be part of the change, let's be agents of God's purposes of restoration.

Definition of Key Terms

- **Loving-kindness:** The original Hebrew word for loving-kindness is *jesed*. It also translates as goodness, constant love, mercy, faithfulness and devotion. It's used 240 times in the Old Testament, especially in the book of Psalms. This term is one of the most important to describe the behavior that God expects from His sons and daughters.

- **Decline:** It's the progressive loss of perfection, a downward path that leads to ruin, a process of deterioration. Moral decline weakens societies, leaving their citizens exposed and vulnerable to all kinds of threats. Moral decline has been the cause of the disappearance of great empires, such as the Roman Empire, for example.

- **Minimalist:** Lifestyle that rejects consumerism and the accumulation of material goods. It focuses on returning to a simple life, acquiring and preserving only what is necessary for daily activities and for living in a comfortable and healthy way. It rejects the idea of luxury, of paying high prices for branded items, of discarding things that are still useful just to follow a fashion or trend.

- **Solidarity:** helps others without expecting to receive anything in return. The supportive person identifies with the needs of the other person and accompanies them on their way so that they can reach their goals.

Summary

Loving-kindness is one of the qualities of God's holy love that we must practice in our lives. It's a selfless love which identifies with those who are in need, provides sincere friendship, and actively engages in the search for solutions. When we practice loving kindness as a church, the kingdom of God draws near and becomes present in our communities. As a result, people trust Christians, open their hearts to Jesus Christ, and lives are restored and communities are transformed.

 **Worksheet**

ACTIVITY 1
Put a check next to the acts of kindness that are frequent in your context:

__ Give up the seat on the bus to an elderly person or pregnant woman.

__ Greet strangers in the street or public places.

__ Thank a public employee who did his job well (police, doctor, teacher, etc.).

__ Give way to a person in a wheelchair or disabled person on the sidewalk.

__ When driving, give way to another vehicle that wants to enter the street when there's a lot of traffic.

__ Help an elderly person carry market bags.

__ Lend a hand to an old woman who descends from the bus or is going down stairs.

__ Help a woman who is alone to change a flat tire on her car.

__ Take care of my neighbor's small child while she goes to an appointment.

__ Deliver a plate of biscuits or a welcome cake to a new neighbor in my neighborhood.

__ Help a classmate who has difficulty understanding a course topic.

__ Leave a good tip to the waiter although he has not provided us with good service.

__ Buy food or clothing for a family in need.

__ Dry around the toilet of the public restroom after use.

__ Give up your place in line to a mother with young children.

__ Guide a customer to find what they need in the competitor's store.

__ Help a young child tie their shoelaces.

__ Pick up trash off the floor and put it in the waste container.

ACTIVITY 2
In groups of three to four, answer the following questions:

a. What are some ways in which poor people in your community are unprotected? (For example: no health insurance.)

b. What are the groups of "invisible" people in your community, those who are unprotected or in extreme poverty? (For example: modern slaves)

c. What kind of help do these people need to get out of their situation of extreme poverty?

d. What could your church do to provide solutions for these people with the human resources you all have?

Worksheet - Lesson 7

ACTIVITY 3
What kind of commitment could you make to help a person or family in your community? Check it off of the following list.

__ Make purchases or do some paperwork for an elderly person.

__ Help with the school expenses of a child or adolescent.

__ Contribute with a monthly food basket.

__ Donate a medicine monthly to a person suffering from a chronic illness.

__ Perform regular maintenance on a neighbor's garden.

__ Care for children of a single mother or father.

__ Pick up children of a working mother from school.

__ Tutor to help children in their studies.

__ Practice some sport with the children or adolescents of the neighborhood.

__ Provide housing for immigrants.

__ Give free guidance on benefits or resources that can be obtained from the government.

__ Transport or accompany an elderly person or person with a disability to medical appointments.

ACTIVITY 4
In groups of two to three, answer the following questions:

a. What reveals the individualistic and materialistic lifestyle that some Christians have?

b. How can we lead our brothers and sisters to practice the generous and supportive lifestyle that distinguishes citizens of the kingdom of God?

c. What do you think about the simple lifestyle? Was Jesus' lifestyle simple?

d. Do you think that Christians should adopt a simpler lifestyle? Do you think that by doing so we could have more financial resources to help those in need?

Worksheet - Lesson 7

ACTIVITY 5
Loving-kindness must be put into practice, and only then will it be visible to those around us. Evaluate your life and make decisions for the future by answering the following questions:

a. What are the activities I could stop doing to have more time to show love in a practical way to people in my community?

b. Is there anyone who has done me any harm? What can I do so that I can see the merciful love of God acting in my life?

c. What changes should I make in my life today to adopt a simpler lifestyle and thus have more resources to help others who are in need?

d. What barriers should I tear down to build relationships of friendship and commitment with one of my neighbors?

e. How can I use my profession or trade to show selfless love to the invisible or defenseless of my community?

_____
_____
_____
_____
_____
_____
_____
_____
_____
_____
_____
_____
_____
_____
_____
_____
_____
_____

Worksheet - Lesson 7

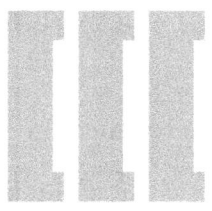

Goodness: Proactive Love
Lesson 8

Lesson Objectives

That the students might...

- **Understand** the difference between charity and kindness.
- **Identify** *acts of kindness that may not be perceived as kind.*
- **Reflect** on the benefits that goodness brings to others.
- **Commit** to develop the good quality of God's love in their lives.

Visual Aids

- Blank pieces of paper.
- Pencils to write with.

Introduction

In the previous lesson, we studied the quality of loving-kindness. Goodness is the next characteristic of the Fruit of the Spirit in Paul's list in Galatians 5:22-23. The Greek word in the original text is *agathosune*, which describes people who are good, virtuous, benevolent, pious and merciful, both in their way of life, and in their treatment of others. Are these characteristics similar? What is the difference between loving-kindness and goodness?

The first describes the kind and supportive aspect of goodness. Goodness is one of the applications of kindness. Goodness is the attitude of giving to others beyond what they need, both spiritually and materially. But goodness also refers to doing good to others, even if it's necessary to be firm and not necessarily using gentle methods.

 Ask students to complete Activity 1.

The word *agathosune* is a Christian term. It's mentioned in the New Testament as a quality of brothers and sisters in the faith who have been regenerated and born into the spiritual life as children of God. Paul, writing to the church in Rome, tells them: *"I myself am convinced, my brothers and sisters, that you yourselves are full of goodness, filled with knowledge and competent to instruct one another."* (Romans 15:14). That is, in the process of the healthy development of the disciple of Jesus, growing in knowledge of the Word and in the practice of goodness must go hand in hand.

In this lesson we'll study some examples of people who are recognized as good in the Bible.

Bible Study

1. THE GOODNESS OF CREATION

The first time that the idea of goodness appears in the Bible is in the account of Creation.

> **Ask the class: How many times does the word "good" appear in Genesis 1:1 to 1:30? What things does God rate as good?**

We notice in this story in verse 30 that at the end of the sixth day after completing His work, the Creator contemplates it, evaluates it and exclaims with great enthusiasm that the whole of His creation was immensely good. The Hebrew word for "good" used here is *tov* which expresses these meanings: kind, cute, fair, morally good, practical, desirable, beautiful. We can summarize the work good in these three ways:

The Fruit-Filled Life

[[[Draw the following graph on the board.]]]

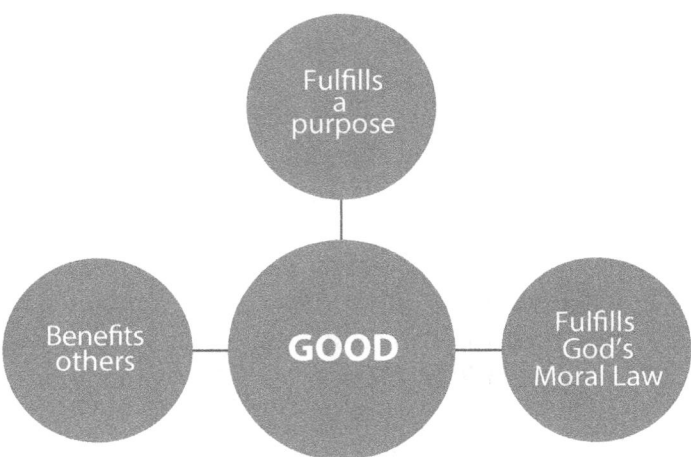

So, to be good in the eyes of God, our life must meet these three requirements. First, God's creation did what God expected. Each of us has been given the gift of life, but along with that gift, we've also been given a purpose within God's plan for His Creation. Our talents and gifts, our personal calling and the passion that God places in our hearts to solve a problem that affects other people, indicate the path that God has chosen for us. When God looks at us and sees us fulfilling His expectations for our life, His heart is filled with joy.

Secondly, the creation reflected the holy nature of the Creator. A good person for God is one who lives in holiness, who has renounced sin, and who no longer has a rebellious heart towards God. The good person lives to please God and therefore doesn't sin against their brother or sister. They are people who distinguish themselves from the rest because they have died to selfishness and always choose to do the right thing in the eyes of their Lord.

[[[Ask a student to read Deuteronomy 30:15. Ask the class: What is the destiny of those who depart from good and choose to do evil?]]]

God rejoices when His children show their true holy nature and choose to do good.

Thirdly, in the original creation, all beings lived in harmony and peace; coexistence provided well-being to all equally. Good people give joy to others. They aren't selfish, have generous hearts, and seek the opportunity to do good to bless the lives of others. When God looks at such a person, He can see their good deeds, and these good actions testify to the goodness in their hearts. God rejoices when His sons and daughters spread love in this world and contribute to the harmonious coexistence of all His creation.

2. JESUS: A GOOD TEACHER

Luke 18:18-30 recounts the encounter between Jesus and a leading man in his community who addressed Jesus and called him "good teacher".

**▐▐▐ Distribute the pieces of paper and pencils to do the activity: "Negotiated Definitions".
Write this phrase on the board: "Jesus was good because ..."
Ask your students to complete the sentence individually.
When they're done, have them get into groups of 2 and "negotiate their ideas"
by writing a single sentence that represents what they both think.
Upon completing this stage, have them get into groups of 4 students (combine 2 groups of 2, each with a definition). Each group will develop a single response to the phrase that represents the ideas of the 2 groups. When the groups finish, complete the sentence on the board with input from all the groups, until you get a phrase that summarizes the thinking of the whole class.
Then read the finished sentence and congratulate the students for their work. ▐▐▐**

We can all agree that Jesus was goodness incarnate. Evidently this man recognized the difference between Jesus and the other rabbis or teachers of his time. The rabbis taught that "there was nothing good outside of the law." Jesus answered, *"Why do you call me good? ... No one is good - except God alone."*

This was a good man in the eyes of his neighbors. He had been obedient to the commandments since he was young; no one could point out any sin in him. For others, this man had already earned eternal life, however, he came to Jesus because he felt that something was missing. He didn't believe that his life was one hundred percent pleasant to the holy God. He asked the question, "What do I have to do to inherit eternal life?"

**▐▐▐ Ask a student to read Luke 18:22-27.
Ask the class: What did this man need to do to be good in God's eyes? ▐▐▐**

Jesus' response demonstrates his knowledge of the human heart. This man's problem wasn't his wealth, but he lived for himself. Wealth was his god; he dedicated all his energy, thought and devotion to it. If he wanted to feel fulfilled in life, he had to learn to live for others with the same passion with which he had lived for himself.

The contrast of Jesus with the teachers of his time can be seen in the parable of the talents in Matthew 25:21.

 **Ask students to complete Activity 2.
Then ask them to share their answers with the rest of the class.**

As we see in these passages, God likes it when we do more than others expect of us. Our goal to do good should never be the average that other people are willing to give. Goodness implies going beyond; it's a proactive love, a love that seeks the opportunity to do the maximum possible good for others.

We see this proactive love over and over again in Jesus' actions. He did things for others even when others criticized him. He did them because they was morally right in God's eyes. Defying the laws of those times, he forgave prostitutes, didn't rebuke the woman with a blood flow that touched him but instead rewarded her by healing her, prevented the woman who had been caught committing adultery from being stoned, healed the sick on the Sabbath, etc. On all occasions when he had to decide how to act, he always put God's moral law first. Again and again he put his life at risk by not following human laws when they went against the will of God. He was also criticized,

The Fruit-Filled Life

misunderstood, or identified as a political extremist. Jesus rebuked anyone who threatened the integral well-being of people. He defeated diseases, expelled demons, rebuked the storm, accused religious leaders and did everything from pure goodness.

Jesus did things that no one expected of him, not because he was superhuman, but because he allowed his life to be a channel through which God's goodness flowed. He surprised people when he multiplied the loaves and fishes, but also when he agonized on the cross and asked his Father for forgiveness for those who had mistreated him (Luke 23:34). In both cases, what motivated Jesus was the same kind and merciful love of God, a love that doesn't care about fulfilling people's expectations, but meets God's expectations.

Guide your students to complete Activities 3 and 4.

3. Joseph of Arimathea

In addition to Jesus, there are two of his disciples whose kindness is recognized in the New Testament Scriptures. The first is Joseph of Arimathea. He played an important role during the burial of Jesus as is mentioned in the four of the gospels:

**Ask four students to read:
Mark 15:43-46, Luke 23:50-53, John 19:38-42 and Matthew 27:57-60.**

Following the details provided by each of the evangelists, we can learn more about the history of Joseph and his relationship with Jesus. Joseph was originally from Arimathea, a city in the province of Judea, about 35 kilometers northwest of Jerusalem. He was an educated and rich man.

Joseph had long been Jesus' disciple, but he was following him in secret, as was Nicodemus, since they were both members of the Council of Jerusalem or Sanhedrin. Both disagreed with the members of this council in their intention to arrest and condemn Jesus. It's likely that they were absent from this meeting that was convened quickly and in the early hours of the morning.

The goodness and justice of Joseph are shown in his courage to appear before Pilate and ask for Jesus' body. In those days, the bodies of criminals that were not claimed by their relatives were left hanging so that the vultures and dogs fed on them, and then they were buried in a mass grave. With the exception of John, the rest of the disciples had looked away from the agony and death of the Lord and had hidden themselves in the upper room. But Joseph, with his act of kindness, saved the body of Jesus from such a horrendous end, thus keeping the dignity of his teacher in his death.

One of the requirements to request the body was to have a sepulcher in Jerusalem. John and the women with Mary, the mother of Jesus, were from Galilee and had no property in the city. Joseph assumed this responsibility and provided a new grave which he had bought for himself and his family. The tomb dug in the rock was a posthumous gift from this disciple to his teacher.

Nicodemus joined Joseph and, following the custom, they prepared the body with aromatic ointments and bandages to place it in the grave. Then Joseph rolled the rock to seal the grave.

What Joseph did by taking care of Jesus' body and giving him an honorable burial was an admirable act for which we remember him even today. His goodness led him to overcome his fears and do what was right in God's eyes.

The Fruit-Filled Life

4. BARNABAS

The next disciple of Jesus whose kindness is mentioned is the man we know as Barnabas. His birth name was Joseph and he was a Levite originally from the island of Cyprus. It was the disciples who gave him the nickname of Barnabas, which means "comforter."

Barnabas was one of the most respected members of the Church in Jerusalem. The first time he is mentioned is in Acts 4:32-37, where we find that he sold a field and brought the money to the apostles to meet the needs of the early community of faith. His generosity and honesty were known to all.

▌▌▌ Ask a student to read Acts 11:22-26. Then ask the class: What other spiritual qualities does Luke, the writer of Acts, mention that Barnabas had? ▌▌▌

Barnabas showed with his actions that he was a person full of the Holy Spirit. Barnabas had an unusual gift, he could see the potential of people, especially in young people. Acts 9:26-31 says that when Paul arrived in Jerusalem to appear before the apostles to join the Church, they didn't want to receive him because they didn't believe in his conversion and were afraid of him. But Barnabas welcomed Paul, heard his story, and was convinced that Jesus had changed Paul's heart. Then he used his influences, especially with James and Peter, to have Paul meet with them. Barnabas introduced Paul and supported his story. As a result, Peter was also convinced and invited Paul to be his guest for two weeks. That was how Paul came to enter the ministerial team of the disciples in Jerusalem. Because of his goodness, Barnabas had the courage to remain with Paul at a crucial time in his Christian life. If Barnabas had not looked after Paul, the story might have been different.

After this, Barnabas, who had been commissioned by the apostles, left for the Church in Antioch which was in the midst of great growth. Many people had become Christians and didn't have teachers and preachers to disciple them in the faith of Jesus (Acts 11:1-22). William Barclay says about this decision: *"By the grace of God they sent whom they sent. They could have sent someone with a rigid and narrow mindset who would have made the law a god and who was bound by its rules and regulations; but they sent the man who had the greatest heart of the whole Church. They sent Barnabas."*

When Barnabas saw what was happening there, and that more and more people of different races and cultures had come to the feet of Christ, he sought the help of someone more prepared than he was. Paul was the person that the new church needed, so Barnabas went and found him and put him in charge of the work. Once again, the goodness of Barnabas is shown in his willingness to step aside to help the church grow.

In chapter 13 verses 1-3, we're told that after some years of ministry, Paul and Barnabas had started several teachers in Antioch. The Church already had spiritual leaders and they were able to start more churches in other cities. At the beginning, Barnabas was the leader of the missionary team, but over time, Paul assumed leadership. Barnabas knew how to step aside and take second place because this favored the advancement of missions. After several years of serving together, Barnabas and Paul separated and were no longer partners in the mission.

▌▌▌ Ask a student to read Acts 15:36-41. Ask the class: What was the reason for this separation? ▌▌▌

The Fruit-Filled Life

Paul felt that he couldn't trust Mark again because he had abandoned them previously. The conflict between Paul and Barnabas was serious and Barnabas didn't yield. Again, we see Barnabas seeing the potential of this young man who needed a second chance. Barnabas defended and accompanied Mark, just as he had done years ago with Paul himself, and took him with him to Cyprus. After this, Barnabas is not mentioned again in the book of Acts. According to tradition, Barnabas was tortured and killed in Cyprus by Jewish enemies of Christians and Mark was able to flee and escape to Alexandria, where he served as a teacher and preacher of the church for several years.

The goodness of Barnabas led him to stand by this young man and devote time to his formation, even when others didn't believe in him. In the following years when Paul was imprisoned in Rome, he acknowledged his mistake and wrote to Timothy: *"Only Luke is with me. Get Mark and bring him with you, because he is helpful to me in my ministry"* (2 Timothy 4:11). Mark proved to be a valuable servant for the church; he also remained by Peter's side during his ministry and became like a son to the apostle (1 Peter 5:13). Mark was also the author of the first gospel to circulate in the churches in those days.

 Guide your students to complete Activity 5.

Definition of Key Terms

- **Proactive:** Person who decides how to act at all times, anticipating events, acting decisively and creatively to solve problems. Someone willing to intervene in a situation, to be of help, without waiting for someone to ask.

- **Sanhedrin:** The great council of Jerusalem consisted of 71 men, all members of prominent Jewish families. Among them were relatives of the high priest, elders and scribes. Under the permission of the Roman Empire, this council judged the important cases and could condemn to death, but this sentence had to be ratified by the Roman procurator.

- **Condescending:** characterized by a patronizing or superior attitude toward others.

- **Permissive:** A person who is excessively tolerant, who easily grants permission to another to do what they want without worrying about the consequences or well-being of that person or those around them.

Summary

Good proactive love is related to fair and generous acts at all times and circumstances of life. It's a goodness which is not influenced by the opinion of others, or by their behavior, but seeks to do things according to God's expectations. The good person makes his own decisions, takes the side of the misunderstood, is patient with the weak and young, believes in the potential of human beings, and accompanies them to reach their best for the kingdom of God.

# Worksheet

ACTIVITY 1
Mark in the following list the situations that you have witnessed in which an act of goodness may not have been received as an act of kindness by the recipient.

__ Vaccinate a young child.

__ Clean an infected wound.

__ Fix a bone out of place.

__ Kill an injured animal to put it out of its misery.

__ Put a very old and sick dog to sleep.

__ Promote policies against the consumption of alcohol or drugs.

__ Avoid the sale of junk food to children in schools.

__ Remove a teenager from bad company.

__ Refuse to sell prescription medicine without a prescription.

ACTIVITY 2
Answer the following questions after reading the indicated passages.

a. Which servants received the qualification as "good and faithful" in Matthew 25:14-28?

b. Why did the servant in the story get punished?

c. How many things do Christians stop doing today because of laziness?

d. What similarity do you find between this parable and James 4:17?

e. What is the relationship between laziness and sin to God?

ACTIVITY 3
Read the following paragraph and then answer: How does this teaching apply to my current situation?

"The goodness of our God must be reflected in our behavior. Ephesians 5:8-10 says: 'For you were once darkness, but now you are light in the Lord. Live as children of light (for the fruit of the light consists in all goodness, righteousness and truth) and find out what pleases the Lord.'

But some confuse being kind with being tolerant or permissive, that is to say, to ignore faults or turn a blind eye to sin. But the Bible teaches that we cannot separate God's mercy from His justice, neither is greater than the other. We should not think that because God is good, we can do whatever we want because we won't be punished anyway."

ACTIVITY 4

Worksheet - Lesson 8

Mention some of the laws of your country that shouldn't govern the lives of Christians since they oppose the moral law of God. The moral law of God is summed up in the 10 commandments. The first 4 refer to loving God and the next 6 to loving others. Jesus summarized the moral law of God in the Greatest Commandment in Matthew 22:37-39.

ACTIVITY 5
Answer the following questions to assess the level of goodness you show in your life. Then write your personal goals to perfect the quality of good love.

a. Which of Jesus' attitudes should we imitate according to 1 Peter 2:21-23? In what areas do I need to practice goodness like Jesus did?

b. What is the example I should follow from the life of Joseph of Arimathea? In what situations will I begin to show the kind of love he did?

c. Which characteristics of love mentioned in 1 Corinthians 13:4 were present in the life of Barnabas? Which one or ones do I need to perfect in my life?

d. In what situations do we need Christians to act to defend the moral values of the kingdom of God?

e. What changes do I need to make in my way of thinking and acting to be a visible instrument of God's goodness in the world?

Worksheet - Lesson 8

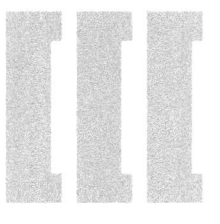

Love that Perseveres
Lesson 9

Lesson Objectives

That the students might...

- **Know** the characteristics of firm, constant, reliable and faithful love.
- **Evaluate** their level of faith or trust in God.
- **Reflect** on the dangers of basing their decisions and actions on their moods.
- **Identify** the areas of their development as disciples where they need a higher level of commitment.

Visual Aids

- Write on 5 pieces of paper or cardboard, in large print, each of the following words: lying, distrust, unbelief, infidelity, indifference.
- On another 5 pieces of paper or cardboard of the same size, another five words: truth, trust, faithfulness, perseverance, certainty.
- Tape the pieces of paper on the board.

Introduction

The next quality of love as a Fruit of the Spirit in the list of Galatians 5:22-23 translates as faithfulness or loyalty and also as faith or trust in God. The Greek term that Paul uses is *pistis* which describes a believing, confident, person of faith, but also a person who is faithful, reliable and trustworthy.

Place on the table the five pieces of paper with the words: lying, distrust, unbelief, infidelity, indifference. Then ask students to form 5 groups and each group choose a word.

 **Guide the students to complete Activity 1. As they finish, ask them to share their answers with the rest of the class.**

Each of these words: lying, distrust, unbelief, infidelity, and indifference have their antonym, that is, a word that describes the opposite attitude or behavior.

Put the other 5 pieces of paper on the table with the words: truth, trust, faithfulness, perseverance, and certainty. Then ask the students to match their word with the word that describes the opposite attitude or behavior. Glue the pairs of opposite words together as indicated below. Add plus and minus symbols and explain to students that the qualities that are in the left column are those that the Spirit wants to add and develop in our lives, while those on the right must be subtracted/discarded from the life of every disciple of Jesus.

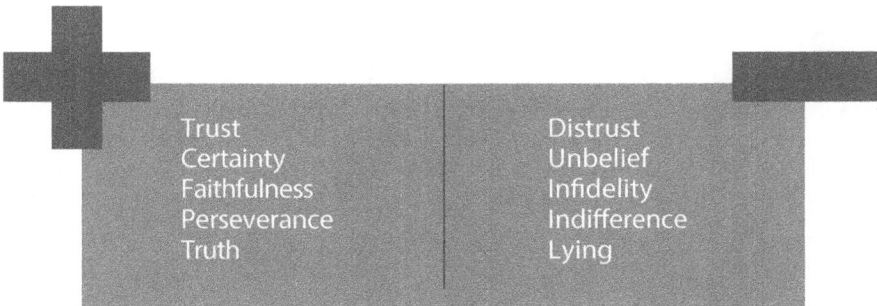

These are the five qualities that must grow in our lives: trust, consistency, faithfulness, perseverance and truth. They are related to the ninth characteristic of the Fruit of the Spirit that we'll study in this lesson.

The Fruit-Filled Life

Bible Study

1. Trust

One of the first lessons we learn in life in general and in the Christian life in particular is to trust others. Building trust in others and in ourselves is essential for healthy mental and emotional development. But it's even more important to learn to trust God. In fact, we cannot grow in the Christian life and cultivate a relationship of love and fellowship with the Creator if we don't learn to trust Him. In Hosea 12:6, he says: *"But you must return to your God; maintain love and justice, and wait for your God always."*

God teaches us to trust Him by demonstrating that he is a trustworthy God, a God who keeps his word.

Ask a student to read Joshua 23:14. Then ask the class: Why did Joshua feel safe?

The life of a Christian is very different when he learns to trust fully in God. However, trusting is not easy for everyone, especially when people have had bad experiences with people who betrayed their trust.

   **Ask students to complete Activity 2.**

As we saw in the passage of Hosea 12:6, we must decide to trust God at all times and in all circumstances. It's when we obey God that we show that we trust Him. Let's take the example of tithing. When we tithe and give generously, God sees that we believe in His promises to supply all that we need (Philippians 4:19).

   Ask students to complete Activity 3.

As we saw in activity 3, the Bible encourages us to place all our trust in God. We cannot love God with all our heart if we don't trust Him. We must cast aside our fears and accept that God is the most reliable being in the universe; He will never let us down.

2. Certainty or faith

The opposite of unbelief is certainty, which we can also call faith. Several levels of faith are experienced in the Christian's life. At the beginning of our experience as Jesus' disciples, we experience saving faith. This is faith, which put into action, makes the penitent person trust fully in Jesus Christ to receive forgiveness for their sins and the promise of salvation.

Ask a student to read Romans 10:8-9. Ask the class: What should a person do to be cleansed of their sins and receive the gift of eternal life?

The only requirement to obtain eternal salvation is to believe and confess.

The second level is faith as a gift. This is the faith that appears in the list of spiritual gifts in 1 Corinthians 12:1-11. The gift of faith refers to a gift from the Spirit that some believers receive which drives them to put into practice a deeper kind of faith than what we normally have. People with this gift of faith achieve great things for God's kingdom, because what sounds impossible to others, they see as possible. Jesus referred to this faith in the parable of the mustard seed.

▌▌▌ Ask a student to read Matthew 17:20. ▐▐▐

We can all develop this faith if we learn to trust God and stop seeing obstacles as barriers impossible to cross.

The third level is faith as fruit. This is the faith that interests us for our study of the Fruit of the Spirit. The Greek word *pistis* means to place all our confidence in the Word of God and what He may do in any circumstance of our lives. The fruit of faith is demonstrated in that assurance that God is with us at all times, that He protects us in every place, that we can fully trust in Him and in His faithfulness to us.

Faith as a Fruit of the Spirit is not just being positive. It enables us to look at people and the future with hope because it helps us have complete confidence that God will fulfill His promises. Faith like this enables us to have joy in the midst of trials; it's what makes us sing praises to God in the midst of difficulties; it's faith that looks beyond circumstances, trusting that God has a purpose for everything and for everyone. It looks beyond everyday events and trusts in the Lord God of history. It pushes us to get involved with everything we are and everything we have in God's restoration plan for humanity, acting with joy and hope in the ministry to which we have been called.

3. FAITHFULNESS AND PERSEVERANCE

Faith should be the Christian's natural response to God's faithfulness. Faith, faithfulness and perseverance go hand in hand; you cannot practice one without the other. But ... how easy is it to practice faithfulness in the times we live in? Nothing around us seems to be stable. Governments change, laws change, people change their minds, languages change, marriages change, technology changes, the markets and the value of currency change. In our context of abrupt change in which we live, it seems that faithfulness has gone out of fashion.

In our consumerist culture, we have learned to value change. Of course, those who benefit from this lifestyle are the companies that want to sell us their products. Why are disposable products so appealing to us? It's simple ... they don't require that we maintain them. If we speak for example of plastic disposal plates, cutlery, glasses, napkins etc. We don't have to wash, dry and store them. We say we prefer these things because it suits us. Similarly, there's little interest in repairing things that are broken; it's easier and faster to buy replacements.

All this adds to environmental pollution, but the problem is that we have learned to treat people in the same way that we value things. Today companies talk about "disposable labor", that is, temporary employees or those who work part time and who receive low salaries and few benefits. Companies aren't committed to their employees, replacing them when they are no longer useful.

Today in the same way that we use disposable things for our convenience, we also easily discard friends, our boy or girl friends, jobs and church. We can see this clearly in the style of relationships that couples assume today. Living under the same roof, without obligations, has become the fashion. The "advantage" is that there are no "ties" or commitment to a long-term relationship. Today, loyalty and faithfulness over a prolonged period of time are perceived as a limitation to individual freedoms.

Also, we don't make the effort to repair broken relationships. When dealing with other people becomes difficult, the easiest thing is to pack up and go elsewhere in the same way as when a product no longer pleases us: we simply look for another. Similarly, when things aren't done in the church as we might like to have it done, we look for another congregation.

The culture of the disposable opposes deep commitments. In our context, the value of committing to something or someone has been lost. We live in a world with an insatiable search for the new, for change, for new experiences, as if we wanted to fill in something we're missing. The idea that something can remain unalterable for a long time doesn't sound real in an environment where everything changes constantly. Faithfulness and commitment seem to be old fashioned customs.

 Ask students to complete Activity 4.

||| Ask students, if they have an internet connection on their cell phone, to search for "Christians without commitment" and see how many sites appear. Then ask the class: How is the escape from the commitment of the culture around us affecting us as Christians? |||

In the environment of extreme individualism in which we live, people want to be free to do what they want with their lives without having ties that limit them. They want to have the freedom to change their minds and choose from several options all the time. They prefer to say ... "I will arrive when I can or I will see if I can go." This is equivalent to saying, "Don't count on me" or, "I'm going if I don't get something better to do during the weekend." With these excuses, we try to appear good outwardly, but we show that we don't really want any commitment to limit our freedom. To maintain our independence and autonomy, we make sure that nobody controls us.

What we see as a result of this elusive behavior are people who feel deeply alone, having a huge emptiness inside them. They ignore the fact that what they need is to cultivate intimate relationships of love, friendship, trust, and that to achieve that they must make long-term commitments.

We were not created to maintain superficial relationships; we need to cultivate deep relationships of fellowship. Evading commitments in relationships makes us sick.

But let's not fool ourselves. It's not possible to be true sons and daughters of God without committing ourselves to faithfulness. Since Old Testament times, believers have known that God responds faithfully to our faithfulness.

||| Ask a student to read Psalms 101:6. |||

The psalmist affirms that God has his eyes on people who are faithful to Him. He has chosen them to serve Him and to live forever with Him. God trusts them because they demonstrate with their actions that they are trustworthy. The faithful are people of impeccable behavior. They aren't perfect since they aren't exempt from making mistakes, but they are complete in their relationship with their Lord and other human beings.

Ask students to complete Activity 5.

Just like us, God prefers to work and live with reliable faithful people.

4. AUTHENTICITY VERSUS CONDITIONAL LOYALTY

Another characteristic of contemporary people is that they follow their emotions. We can see around us people who think they are authentic, but they make decisions based on their moods. The result is that people only do something if they "want" to do it. They say things like: "I'll go to church if I feel like it" or "I'll clean up later when I feel like it." Do these phrases sound familiar?

When this happens, we're being loyal to ourselves, but this kind of loyalty is not governed by principles or values that we have adopted for our life. We're just following our feelings and moods.

Another way we're taught to practice loyalty in contemporary culture is by behaving in a certain way, following the "rules of the game." For example, it's assumed that if I lie for a friend, I show my loyalty to him. It's acceptable that I do something illegal in the company if it's the way the bosses expect me to prove my loyalty. Hopefully, friends will cover for us and support us in everything, for example in deceiving our mother, our girlfriend or the teacher. Those are considered loyal friends. However, if a friend tells us that she won't support us, we doubt her loyalty and the quality of her friendship.

Saul and Samuel also lived in a context of great changes. A new form of government was being established in Israel while they were still living in the middle of the war over the conquest of Canaan. God's way of speaking with His people was changing. Samuel was the last judge and also the first prophet. However, there was a big difference between Saul and Samuel, and this was because of their commitments on which both based their decisions.

Ask a student to read 1 Samuel 13:1-13.

In this passage we see that Saul was a king without firm commitments. Like many people today, his moods guided his decisions and actions. Saul's actions, guided by his impulses, led his entire family to destruction and put the other families of his nation at grave risk. Let's not fool ourselves, everything we do in our lives has repercussions.

5. THE CULTIVATION OF A FAITHFUL CHURCH

Evangelical churches continue to grow rapidly throughout the world. Between 1900 and 2000, evangelicals have grown 122 percent in the world, while the Catholic church has only grown 6 percent and the Orthodox church has decreased 50 percent. This is due to the great commitment and faithfulness that the Evangelical churches have shown with evangelism, Christian compassion and church planting in other cultures, especially in the last 200 years.

However, the evangelical churches have a great weakness; they aren't every deep spiritually. In our world today, most Christians suffer from spiritual illiteracy. Today we face one of our greatest challenges in the history of the Church, which is to train this immense number of believers so that they become mature and committed to holy living. But this problem can only be solved if spiritual leaders commit themselves to the formation of God's people instead of focusing solely on attractive programs to appeal to and entertain a crowd. When churches aren't committed to the task of making disciples, they will be weak, unstable, and worldly. Today God is calling leaders to fulfill the main function to which he has called them.

**[[[Ask a student to read Ephesians 4:11-16. Then ask the class:
What is the main responsibility that God has called church leaders to do?]]]**

The purpose of the Christian life is to learn to live in holiness, following Jesus' model. This is the Great Commission that Jesus entrusted to his church and is the primary call to leadership. Our evangelism programs should lead people to make a commitment to progressive discipleship so they can have firm spiritual foundations on which to build their lives and ministries.

6. THE CULTIVATION OF LOVE THAT PERSEVERES

As we have seen in the previous points, this virtue of faithful love is not well understood and practiced by people in our day. However, Jesus' disciples have a responsibility to develop this quality as one of the Fruit of the Spirit.

There are four characteristics of faithfulness that we need to cultivate in our lives.

[[[Show students the graph "The Cultivation of Love that Perseveres" in Activity 6.]]]

We can see in this graph how the church, through a discipleship process, guides the new believer to make commitments to Jesus Christ, his people, and his mission. We also observe in the second column of the graph the five commitments that we're responsible to teach to new believers so that they become firm, constant, reliable and faithful Christians:

a). Commitment to live as holy disciples of Jesus, with solid roots in the Word of God (Colossians 2:5-7).

b). Commitment to the local church and its leadership. They need to learn to be constant in their attendance, tithes and offerings.

c). Commitment to the work of God in the world. They need to learn how to consecrate their lives to the service of God, serving others through the use of their spiritual gifts and according to their individual calling.

d). Commitment to their own development and integral training to carry out a ministry of excellence for God, his people and the world.

············o **Conclude the class with Activity 7 and a time of commitment and prayer.**

Definition of Key Terms

- **Authenticity** is the quality of being genuine or real. People who show themselves to be what they are; whose identity and lifestyle are true and consistent with their values and beliefs.
- **Certainty** is the state of being free from doubt or reservation; confident; sure; an assured fact.
- **Consumer culture:** The lifestyle of acquiring and accumulating goods, which aren't always necessary, in an exaggerated way. Today, many marriages are destroyed and many people live in debt through the irresponsible use of credit cards used to acquire unnecessary products, just to get the latest model or to follow the fashions. **Disposable:** The consumer lifestyle is associated with throwing away different products after maybe only using them once, causing serious ecological problems.
- **Indifference:** is a lack of interest or concern in something; to consider something or someone as unimportant.
- **Faith as a gift:** The gift of faith is the ability to put trust in God, to miraculously meet real needs, with the firm assurance that a response will be received. It's not an irrational faith, but one that's based on God's promises, on the knowledge of his love, and on the conviction that as people and as a church, we're serving according to God's plan and asking according to his will (Matthew 17: 20). Christians with the gift of faith have the ability to encourage others to trust and wait for divine provision in a given situation.
- **Reliable:** People who can be trusted because they speak truthfully and are loyal or faithful.
- **Faithfulness:** Unfailingly remaining loyal to someone or something. Faithfulness implies punctuality or responsibility in the execution of responsibilities.
- **Individualism:** It's the tendency to think and act independently, without subjecting oneself to current norms or customs, either in society or in a group of people. This position defends the individual's rights over the rights of all others. The origin of this word comes from uniting the terms "individual" and "ism", that's why individualistic thinking is related to the sins of selfishness, vanity, self-endorsement, and rebellion against divine authority.
- **Loyalty:** loyal people demonstrate constant fidelity, for example to another person, to a cause or to a purpose in their life. They are honorable, conducting themselves always within certain norms and principles that they have chosen to adopt.
- **Persevering:** Someone who is persevering continues firmly in a course of action in spite of difficulty or opposition. Persevering Christians walk with Christ until the end of their lives (Hebrews 12:1). Maintaining a relationship with God every day is the responsibility of believers, since if they neglect their relationship with God, they can fall back into the life of sin and lose their salvation (1 Corinthians 9:27).

Summary

This quality of the Fruit of the Spirit can be summed up in faithfulness, which is the opposite of distrust, unbelief, infidelity, indifference and lies. Today it's difficult to develop this spiritual quality in the midst of a consumerist and individualistic cultures that evade long-term commitments and push people to make decisions based on their moods, rather than based on the eternal values and principles of God's Word. To cultivate faithfulness in our lives, we need to put all our trust in God, who has given us enough reasons and evidence of His faithfulness. Today the Christian church needs Christians committed to the life of holiness, to the mission of God and to their local church. A church without commitment is invisible to the world. But a church formed in a process of progressive discipleship won't only live in holiness, but will transform the world, serving others in love. The Christian life that pleases God is one that assumes deep and permanent commitments, that perseveres in loving God, and that loves and serves others.

 # Worksheet

ACTIVITY 1
To be completed in groups. Write the word you have chosen on the line and then answer the questions.

- ¿How common is _____ in the people of your community?

- Can you mention any occupation or profession in which the practice of _____ is more common?

- Have you witnessed an occasion when a Christian also practices it? _____
_____

ACTIVITY 2
Complete the following activity to assess your current "Level of trust in God." Mark an x in the column that corresponds to your answer. Add the amount of x's in each column and then read the recommendations below for each result.

	Never	Sometimes	Always
I believe that what God says will always be fulfilled in my life.			
I feel confident that I can trust God to control my future.			
I trust that God is always by my side and never leaves me.			
When I pray I ask God to do his will.			
I think that God loves me the same way he loves others.			
I think that God loves me even with my failures and imperfections.			
I believe that God is the person who understands me best.			
I trust that because I tithe, God will provide everything I need.			
I place my burdens on God, trusting that he will do his best.			
I believe that God has cleansed all my sins and will give me eternal life.			
TOTAL			

Worksheet - Lesson 9

Evaluation of the results:

- *Most of the x in the "Always" column.* Your trust in God is strong, but check if there are areas in which you need to mature and get to work on it.

- *If the majority are in the "Sometimes" column.* You will have to work on these specific areas and make decisions to believe in God in a full way from now on. Change the way you think in areas where you have a weakness to trust. Obey God, even if you don't "feel" much trust, and wait to see how God keeps his promises.

- *If the majority are in the "Never" column.* Study in the Bible the evidences and proofs of God's faithfulness. Make the decision to start each day by reading a promise from God to you in the Bible, repeat it whenever you can, and memorize it. Pray that you would believe in God and in His Word, and ask God to increase your faith and trust in Him. Reject any idea of doubt or distrust that Satan brings to your mind. Avoid talking with people who bring you insecurity or sow doubts in you about God's faithfulness. Talk with brothers and sisters whose faith is strong to discover how they cultivated that trust in God and learn from their experiences.

ACTIVITY 3
Complete this activity in pairs. Read the following Bible passages and make a list of some of the reasons we have for trusting God.

a. Psalm 91:9-11 _____

b. Romans 5:8, 8:34 _____

c. Hebrews 13:8 _____

d. Psalms 18:17 _____

e. Ephesians 5:2 _____

f. Jeremiah 29:11 _____

g. Isaiah 12:2 _____

h. 1 Corinthians 10:13 _____

ACTIVITY 4
In groups of three to four students answer the following questions:

a. How does the disposable culture that surrounds us affect us as a church?

_____

_____

b. How does it affect the church that people evade commitment today?

_____

_____

Worksheet - Lesson 9

ACTIVITY 5
Complete in groups of three to four students. The following list includes some life situations in which we need to trust another person. Write in the second column: What quality or qualities would you look for in that person? Then answer the questions below

Situation or Need	Ethical or moral quality or qualities
Leave my little boy or girl in their care.	
Remodel my home.	
Form a business partnership.	
Entrust them with private matters and ask for advice.	
Repair the engine of my car.	
Take care of my plants or my pet when I travel.	

a. Could you say that these qualities describe a faithful person?

b. In our contexts, is it easy to find people worthy of our trust?

c. Do you remember any recent crime that involves one or more people who were not reliable?

d. Has anyone you trusted let you down?

ACTIVITY 6
Graph: The Cultivation of Love that Perseveres

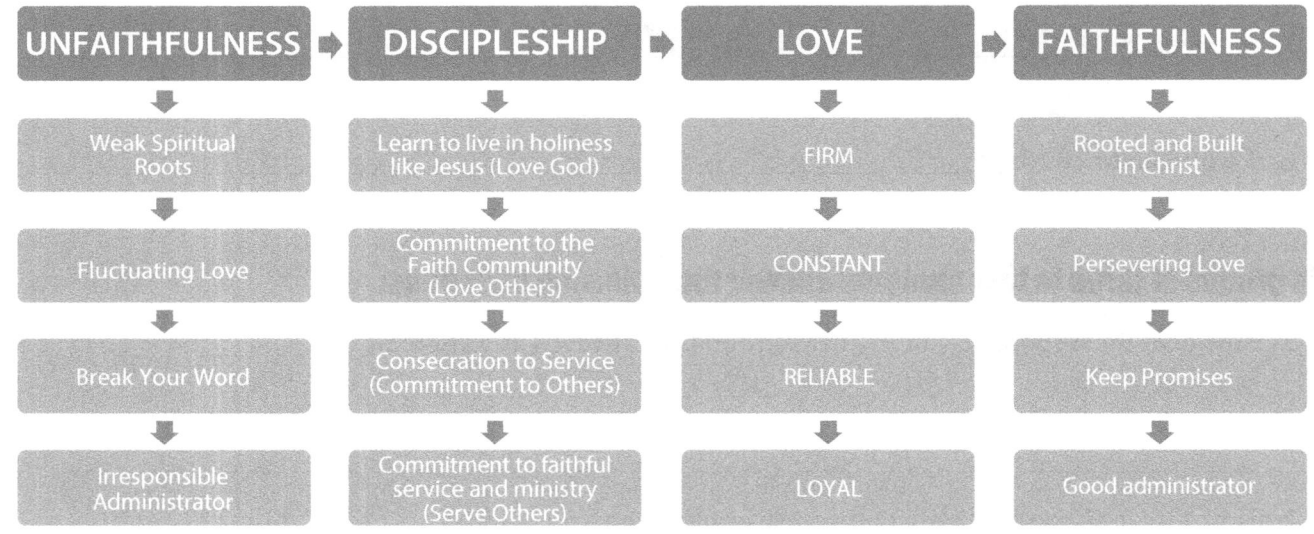

ACTIVITY 7
Evaluate your life by answering the following questions. Then in pairs have a time of prayer to reaffirm your commitment to the Lord.

a. According to Revelation 2:10, faithfulness has a prize in eternity. Look at the 4 characteristics of faithfulness in the last column to the right of the graph of activity 6 and answer: If today you were in the presence of God and your life was evaluated, in your opinion ... would you be approved by God? What should you do from now on to meet God's expectations for your life?

b. Read Matthew 25:21 and reflect: Have you set conditions for God for your faithfulness? Have you been willing to serve God only when things are done your way? Have you stopped tithing and giving generously when your finances are not going well? If your answer to any of these questions is 'yes', you have shown signs of lack of faith and have not been faithful as God expects from His sons and daughters. What will you do about it?

c. What changes should you make in your life so that God and the people around you can fully trust you?

d. Observe the 4 commitments to which discipleship should lead us and respond: Do any of these areas need to be reinforced in your life? Have you postponed any of these goals and commitments? What decisions does God expect of you today?

Worksheet - Lesson 9

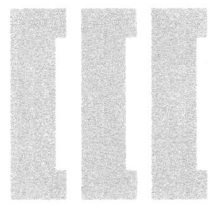

Love that Produces Meekness
Lesson 10

Lesson Objectives

That the students might...

- **Appreciate** Jesus' model of humility.
- **Understand** that we need to give up pride to love our opponents.
- **Value** how Jesus treated his enemies.
- **Practice** acting meekly and humbly in relationships.

Visual Aids

- A bag of peanuts in their shells.
- A giant mallet of those used in masonry to demolish walls or crush things (if you can't get one, use a printed or projected image).
- Bibles as books or on cell phones.
- Judge if you need to use dictionaries for Activity 3.

The Fruit-Filled Life

Introduction

Jesus began his message to the crowd, in the Sermon on the Mount, with a series of promises. Some of these blessings were intended for people who suffered from different causes. But other rewards were intended for people who showed the character qualities of a true son or daughter of God.

> **Ask students to read Matthew 5:1-12 and identify: What are the character qualities that will be rewarded? What will be the reward in each case?**

As we see most of the rewards promised by Jesus are for those who show certain qualities of character such as the poor in spirit, meekness, being merciful, those with clean of hearts and the peacemakers. The interesting thing is that all these qualities cannot be achieved by our personal effort. For example, to get God's forgiveness, we need to humble ourselves before God and recognize our spiritual poverty. Our spirits need to be quickened and given new life by the Lord. This is the only way can we be citizens of the Kingdom of Heaven. In the same way, we cannot cleanse sin from our hearts, only God can give us a new and clean heart. But, once our heart is cleansed, we're responsible to turn away from all kinds of evil and keep our life free of sin.

We have already studied how love helps us to be peacemakers and merciful, qualities of the Fruit of the Spirit. But there's another quality, which has a special reward "the inheritance of the earth." Another characteristic of God's love is meekness, which the Spirit wants to perfect in our lives.

The Greek word that Paul uses in Galatians 5:23 is *prautes*, which in several biblical versions translates as humility. The original Greek term describes a humble, modest and submissive attitude before God. Seen in the person who shows sweetness, goodness and softness in their treatment of others. The meek person is attentive, courteous and willing to serve others in the most humble tasks. In studying this lesson, we'll understand more about this quality of the Fruit of the Spirit through looking at Jesus' example.

Bible Study

1. Jesus' humble attitude towards the Father

Jesus is our best example of meekness and humility of heart. The apostle Paul describes this quality of the Lord's character in the wonderful passage of Philippians 2: 5-11.

 **Ask students to complete Activity 1.**

The only way to cultivate a humble attitude before God is to set aside our pride. Jesus gave up all personal ambition, the desire to achieve fame and prestige, and humbling himself became a man.

Once we put our pride to one side, our hearts are ready to embrace God's will for our lives. Jesus Christ submitted himself to the perfect will of his father and to fulfill the mission God had entrusted to him, out of love of us. We cannot get love out of the equation, for it's the redeeming love of the Father that permeated the Son, who moved them to make the greatest sacrifice to save their beloved creatures.

The apostle Paul explains in Philippians 2: 7, that the Lord stripped himself. The Greek verb that the apostle uses is *kenoun*, which means emptying. Jesus emptied himself of his glory to come to be born as a human being. In 2 Corinthians 8:9 says: *"For you know the grace of our Lord Jesus Christ, that though he was rich, yet for your sake he became poor, so that you through his poverty might become rich."*

That is, Jesus left behind his glory in heaven and became one of us. He voluntarily submitted to hunger, cold, disease, be treated violently and be belittled. None of this would have happened if he had presented himself to us in his glorious divinity. Jesus renounced his divine privileges, and it was this attitude that allowed him to "take the form of a servant," that is, a slave, to offer humanity a service that only the holy Son of God could perform: pay the price for our Sin on the cross, settle our debts with God and give us the gift of eternal life.

Philippians 2:8 continues to speak of the humility of Christ and his absolute submission to the will of his Father. At the moment before he was arrested, Matthew tells us that Jesus was sorely distressed in prayer in the garden of Gethsemane.

Ask a student to read Matthew 26: 36-46.

We don't know the content of most of Jesus' intimate prayers with his Father, but surely one of the things he sought was that his will be always subject to the will of God, so that his life would be useful to his purposes. He also taught us to pray in this way: *"Your will be done on earth as it's in heaven"* (Matthew 6:10).

The context of Paul's passage to the Philippians was the lack of unity among the members of the church. The humble attitude is the cement that unites people, the church, and families. The worst enemy of unity, is self-exaltation, when pride takes control of our emotions and our actions. It's not possible to obey God and serve Him with a proud heart. If we want to be God's children we must love him with all our hearts, with all our minds, with all our soul and all our strength (Mark 12:30). Since Old Testament times God declares that we sin against Him when our pride rebels against His will (Proverbs 21: 4).

We see this same humble and meek character in the Holy Spirit. The lack of selfishness in the Trinity is evident in the relationship between the Father, the Son and the Spirit. There's no competition of powers, there's no struggle to gain popularity. The Spirit is a servant par excellence, doing multiple tasks for our well-being and salvation. He is the one who attracts us to the love of God, who gives us new birth, gives us gifts, fills us with the love of God, is our teacher and also our memory aid! (John 14:26) Like Jesus Christ, He doesn't seek glory for himself, but for the Son and the Father. Wouldn't it be wonderful if human beings practiced this quality of love in our family, in our church and in our society?

2. THE MEEKNESS OF JESUS IN HIS TREATMENT OF OTHERS

To understand meekness better we need to see it in action in Jesus' life. During his time on this earth Jesus related to all kinds of people: rich, poor, people of different professions and trades, people with diseases or who were suffering from different causes, highly educated people and illiterate people. He dealt with people who were friendly to him, who loved and respected him, and also with people who attacked and persecuted him, with people who betrayed him and with soldiers who tortured him to death. But the meekness of the Lord surfaced in dealing with all of them, even with his enemies.

If there was a man in history, who had all the power to destroy his enemies, that was Jesus. What would we do if we had all the power to make others do what we want?

 Ask students to complete Activity 2.

When the Son of God breaks into history, he didn't do so with the power of military force, or of wealth or knowledge, or of a position. The magicians arrived from the east looking for a king and what they found was a baby born in a family of humble workers. Jesus began his ministry with a humble attitude asking John to baptize him, recognizing the importance of his role and his spiritual authority.

Jesus didn't need to take care of his image, because he was genuine, he was not acting a part for people. He was not bothered about being surrounded by the weak and marginalized, sick people, widows, prostitutes, poor, children, or tax collectors.

He was seen as a person who taught with authority, healed the sick and could have entered Jerusalem as a winning king, but he chose to enter sitting on a simple donkey. He washed the disciples' feet, taking the place of a slave. When he was arrested, he allowed them to torture and insult him, without giving resistance or using his power.

When the apostle John in the book of Revelations sought the mighty and triumphant lion, who was worthy to open the seals that would bring God's judgment on earth he could not find it. But what he saw, before God's throne was a lamb. John tells us that all heaven burst into a song of praise: *"Worthy is the Lamb, who was slain, to receive power and wealth and wisdom and strength and honor and glory and praise!"* (Revelation 5:12). A servant God? A meek God? What kind of God do we Christians have?

 **Ask students to complete Activity 3.**

In activity number 3 we have seen that Jesus' treatment with all people was always respectful. Although from our perspective it may seem to us that on occasion, Jesus insulted his enemies. But when we compare the intentions of his enemies and the motives behind Jesus' words, we realize that Jesus didn't respond to the attacks he received selfishly, defensively or with hidden intentions. Let's see some examples:

The Fruit-Filled Life

▌▌▌ **Ask several students to read the following passages: John 7:47, Matthew 12:38, Luke 11:53, Mark 12:13, John 12:19, Matthew 12:14, Luke 16:14, 6:7; Mark 2:18-24, Matthew 12:24.** ▌▌▌

The gospels widely relate the malicious attitude and disrespectful treatment that the religious of the time gave Jesus.

a. They tried to put people against them (John 7:47).

b. They set him up to catch him out; they tried to accuse him and bring him to trial (Matthew 12:38, 22:15, 19:3, John 8:3-5).

c. They harassed him with questions when he was tired, seeking to confuse him (Luke 11:53).

d. They provoked him by asking him to do signs or miracles (Mark 12:13, Matthew 16:1).

e. They were jealous and therefore wanted to destroy his ministry (John 12:19).

f. They conspired in secret to set him up (Matthew 12:14, 22:34, John 11:47) and then to kill him (Mark 3: 6).

g. They mocked Jesus (Luke 16:14) and murmured behind his back (Luke 15:2, John 9:16).

h. They followed him to spy on him and sent undercover spies (Luke 6:7, 20:20-21).

i. They accused him of being false, of deceiving people, of not respecting God's law (Mark 2:18-24, 7:1-5; Luke 6:2, John 9:16), of associating with sinners, sharing his sinful conduct (Mark 2:16) and even went to the extreme of accusing him of serving Satan (Matthew 12:24).

Now let's look at the attitude and the way Jesus treated them.

▌▌▌ **Ask several students to read: Mark 8:5, Luke 11:42-43, 10:25-37.** ▌▌▌

a. Jesus denounced them, Jesus' concern was the people, to whom these confused leaders were not leading the people in the way God expected (Matthew 23:1-37, Mark 8:15).

b. He warned them repeatedly about their wrong behavior and their wrong way of thinking about God's will for His people (Matthew 23:13, Luke 11:42-43).

c. He taught them through illustrations and parables, through asking questions, a method used by teachers at that time. He gave them opportunities to learn activities to help them to understand their error and change their attitude (Luke 10:25-37, 14:1-34).

We can understand Jesus' authoritative treatment of them because, as the Son of God, his motivation was to defend his people against the confusing teachings and bad examples they received from the religious of the time, who, as Luke 16:14 says, had been side tracked from their mission, because they "loved money." However, Jesus not only reproached them for their sin, at the same time when he caught their attention, he was a humble and compassionate teacher, trying to make them understand how far they were from the will of God.

Jesus loved his enemies and was willing to die on the cross for them, but at the same time, with a firm character, he didn't allow them to deny his identity and belittle his ministry.

3. MEEKNESS IS NOT WEAKNESS

People today think that being gentle, meek and humble, is a sign of weakness. In the gospels we see that people were amazed that Jesus didn't use his power to destroy his enemies.

> **Take out the peanut bag and put one on the table. Ask several students to make the attempt to crush the peanut with the mace, but stop at the right time, so as to cause no damage to the shell. They may not succeed on the first attempt, but encourage them to continue until they manage to control the weight of the club and thus not cause damage to the seed. Then as a prize, distribute the peanuts to the class, ask them to break the shell gently so as not to damage the seed. Then ask students: What can we learn about meekness with this illustration?**

How many of us since childhood were taught that the world is like a jungle and that to survive in it we have to be strong? In the society around us, people who have power and strength are admired. Actors with large muscles or with skills in combat arts rare often our favorites. The same goes for video games or computer games, where the use of brute force and violence add points.

> **Ask students to mention examples of action movies or video games that use violence and brute force to take revenge on enemies or to fight evil.**

In today's world everyone wants to be seen as a powerful lion, nobody wants to be compared to a meek lamb. When they attack us, we react by demonstrating our strength, we become tough, we expected men to be "macho men."

We have learned to be aggressive to survive. Women don't want to be submissive to men, young people don't want their parents to govern them, employees fight because their abilities aren't being recognized; They want to "shine" more than their peers so as to get promoted, to obtain a position that gives them power and status. Just look at the photos of selfies on social networks to get a taste of how we promote ourselves to others. People feel they need to be admired, congratulated, recognized and praised by others.

We have been taught to hide our emotions and feelings as culture tells us showing them implies weakness. Showing tenderness to others, crying, and letting our human frailty be seen, is considered typical of "the weaker sex." Service occupations like nursing and caring for children and the elderly, were for a long time "jobs" for women. But since the so-called feminist liberation, women have adopted harder attitudes so as to be seen in the workplace as able to work hard and compete with men for jobs.

However, Jesus' disciples shouldn't be guided by cultural norms but rather look at Jesus and follow his example. Developing a humble and meek character doesn't mean that we don't value ourselves. It doesn't mean keeping quiet in moments of injustice, or accepting abuse and ill-treatment from other people. On the contrary, because we know the value of our life for God, we must react with kindness even if we're treated unfairly, even if others don't value us or don't value what we do.

 Guide the students to complete Activity 4

In the roles in which we Christians serve in leadership at home, in the church and in society, we sometimes need to speak with authority and firmness so that people understand or correct what they might be doing wrong. That's why Paul told Titus, who was a bishop on the island of Crete: *"These, then, are the things you should teach. Encourage and rebuke with all authority. Do not let anyone despise you."* (Titus 2:15)

4. MEEKNESS IN EVERYDAY LIFE

Seeing Jesus' example, we have only to ask ourselves, is it possible for us, the disciples of Jesus, to practice this quality of humble and meek love, even with people who treat us badly and cause us harm?

[[[Ask a student to read Matthew 11:29.]]]

In this passage, Jesus affirms that if we follow him and learn from him, we'll develop a meek and humble character. We're born with proud hearts but we can learn to be meek. Let's look at three things we can do to practice humility in our daily lives:

a). Love and pray for those who persecute us

If there's a mandate that Jesus left us that's difficult to apply, it's this. The Jews in Jesus' time were in the habit of applying the law of "an eye for an eye and a tooth for a tooth." When someone did something against another person, nobody considered that the person who returned the blow did something wrong in God's eyes. But in the new kingdom of justice inaugurated by Jesus, the treatment of enemies is to be totally different.

Jesus taught us to love and pray for those who aren't kind to us: *"But I tell you, love your enemies and pray for those who persecute you, that you may be children of your Father in heaven. He causes his sun to rise on the evil and the good, and sends rain on the righteous and the unrighteous"* (Matthew 5:44-45). What kind of love does the Lord talk about? There's no way that spontaneous affection for people who hurt us is a natural human reaction. This is true and God knows it, and He's not asking us to do anything that's unnatural, since it's not right to love our enemies in the same way that we love our loved ones. The love that Jesus asks us to practice with our enemies is not the kind of love that's born from our heart, that affectionate love we feel for our family. Remember that Greeks had different verbs to differentiate the types of love. In this passage, Jesus uses the verb "agape" that describes a love that's grounded in good will, in a decision to love those who "don't like us" or who treat us badly.

Agape love is a love that doesn't seek revenge or punishment, but seeks the best for the other person, even if it means discipline. Instead of causing harm, this love wants to heal people and find a positive way out of the conflict. This is more than just refraining from returning evil for evil. Agape is a love that acts, which does its best to restore broken relationships.

Although this is difficult to do, the Lord tells us that in order to be authentic children of the Father, we must pray for those who offend us. Does it make any difference in our attitude when we pray for our enemies? The answer is YES and a lot. As Philip Kenneson explains: *"Praying for other people softens our hearts towards them and encourages us to treat them better, like other fallible creatures made in the image and likeness of God."*

When we get angry with others, we're overwhelmed by a feeling of pride, which flows from our wounds. We tell ourselves that we're better than the other person. But if we avoid reacting defensively and seek to be face to face with God, we can see ourselves as we are, in our sin, imperfection and fragility, and also remember God's grace towards us. That gives us a sense of humility and a feeling of compassion for other people.

b). Resist the temptation to always win

In life we cannot avoid conflicts with other people, but for Christians, the way to deal with them and resolve them must be different. One of the things that prevents people from resolving their differences is always wanting to be right. This is clearly seen in the family or when we work as a team. We shouldn't be offended if our idea is not approved, but we must learn to listen to other opinions and value the ideas of others.

To develop a meek character, we need to learn to share our opinions with humility and with the confidence that God will lead us to make the right decision. Because of their temperament, many people find it very difficult to give up control and authority over other people, to accept that things can be done differently, and that not everything should be done "our own way." But temperament should never be used as an excuse to be impolite or rude in dealing with other people.

While we're learning to be humble and meek, we must recognize when we make mistakes. The Spirit will be in charge of letting us know when we have offended someone, and we must have the courage to humbly seek forgiveness for the way we reacted.

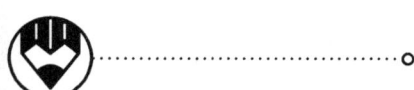 **Ask students to complete Activity 5.**

Definition of Key Terms

- **Meekness:** Humble disposition of the heart before God and other people. It's demonstrated in being kind and respectful, in the refusal to return evil for evil, in seeking to restore relations and ensuring the well-being of the aggressor.
- **Humility:** Refers to the attitude of the person, not to their economic condition. This attitude is that of a friend who stands side by side, doesn't feel superior to others, even if their position or social status allows it. Humility also implies an attitude of service towards others, of considering others as better than oneself.
- **Servant:** The Greek words for servant are diakonos, servant, and doulos, slave, indicate submission of one person to the service of another.
- **Pharisees and Sadducees:** Very zealous of religion, religious leaders of Jewish society in Palestine. They confronted Jesus on many occasions. Along with the Scribes, they considered themselves guardians of the law of Moses and responsible for preserving the customs of the people of Israel.

Summary

Jesus provides us with a perfect model of the quality of meek and humble love that God wants us to develop in our lives. This love is not only put into practice in the way we relate to our loved ones, but also in our relationships with those who mistreat us with their words and their actions. Loving people who don't like us doesn't flow spontaneously from our heart, but comes from our willingness to be kind to everyone. Christians must put aside pride and resist the temptation to always win so that we can constructively solve problems in our relationships. Seeking peace with all and seeking the best for others is the attitude that should govern our relationships.

# Worksheet

ACTIVITY 1
In groups of three, read Philippians 2: 5-11 and answer the following questions.

a. Why does Paul say that Jesus voluntarily lowered himself?

b. What is the relationship between the humiliation of Jesus and his obedience to the Father?

c. Who received the glory for the humiliation and obedience of Jesus Christ?

d. What reward did Jesus receive for his humble and obedient attitude to the Father?

ACTIVITY 2
Answer the following questions:

a. If God granted you the power to make other people obey you, how would you use it? Give three examples.

_____

_____

_____

b. What would people think if they saw a person who has all the power to take revenge on his enemies, but doesn't use it?

_____

_____

ACTIVITY 3
In groups of two or three students, look for the following passages in the Bible and then complete the columns in the box below. To describe Jesus' treatment of a person, use adjectives such as tender, kind, affectionate, sensitive, friendly, understanding, paternal, compassionate, warm, affectionate, courteous, gentle, respectful, repressive, sincere, truthful, authoritative, among others.

Passage	People	Friend or Enemy?	How did Jesus treat them?
John 11:33-44			
Matthew 8:2-4			
Matthew 9:9-13			
John 8:2-11			
Luke 7:37-50			
Matthew 15:1-9			

Worksheet - Lesson 10

ACTIVITY 4
Answer the following questions:

a. Have you ever been mistreated or belittled by another person?

b. Has anyone ever belittled your talents and/or your work?

c. How did you react?

d. What place did pride play in your reaction?

e. How did you continue your relationship with that person after your reaction?

f. Now that you know Jesus' example about what it means to be meek and humble, would you do something different if that happens again?

ACTIVITY 5
Answer the following questions:

a. From today on, how will you apply the recommendations of the apostles Paul (Ephesians 4:26) and James about relationships (James 3:17)?

b. What needs to be transformed in our character so that we treat others meekly and humbly like Jesus?

c. Mention three things you will do from today to further develop the quality of meekness in your life.

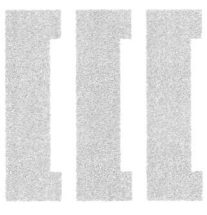

Love that Produces a Balanced Life
Lesson 11

Lesson Objectives

That the students might...

- **Identify** the dangers of an undisciplined life.
- **Understand** that Jesus Christ came to give us complete freedom over sin.
- **Propose** paths of action so as not to fall into the culture of sexual debauchery.
- **Write** a plan to grow towards a comprehensive balance in their life.

Visual Aids

- Two English dictionaries (or consult a search engine on the internet, or on cell phones).
- Two printed images of athletes known in your country for their achievements and Olympic awards or medals. One should be of someone who has stayed away from drugs and other addictions. The other of an athlete who has fallen into vices or addictions and because of this, could not continue with their profession.
- Twelve cards. Write on some of them synonyms for self-control: ABSTINENCE, STABILITY, AUSTERITY, DISCIPLINE, MODERATION, TEMPERANCE. On others write antonyms of self-control: WANTONNESS, EXCESS, UNCONSTRAINT, SELF-INDULGENCE, LICENTIOUSNESS, DECADENCE. All cards must be mixed and made of paper and the same color ink.
- If you're going to use the board, you'll need tape to stick the images and cards to it.
- Sweets or mints to use as a reward (enough for the whole group).

Introduction

For every Christian virtue, there's the opposite behavior. For example, we can choose to speak with the truth or speak with deception or lies. We can choose to forgive or on the contrary we can choose to hate and hold a grudge. The same goes for each of the qualities of love, as the Fruit of the Spirit, and the eighth and final quality mentioned in Galatians 5: 22-23, is no exception.

The word for this lesson, *egkrateía* in Greek, is the one Paul chose to describe this quality. The best translation of this word for us today is self-control, or temperance. *Egkrateía* describes a balanced life that comes as the fruit of the work of the Spirit in the life of Christ's disciples.

To understand the meaning of this quality of love better, we'll define and identify some behaviors that describe it as well as what it's not.

Place photos of athletes on the board or on a large table, separated from each other. Then instruct students to identify these people. Ask students to divide into two groups and distribute half of the cards, already mixed, to each group. Ask students to examine the cards and consult the dictionary to understand their meaning. Then each group, interspersed, will place a card around one of the photos. Explain to the class that the word should describe the behavior of this athlete. Then check together if the cards were well placed. Congratulate the students for the work done and distribute the sweets as prizes.

As we saw in this activity, we're easily seduced and enslaved by pleasures and desires. Today many people think that living a life without sin is impossible. That's why there are still Christians who allow themselves some 'little sins' from time to time. But Jesus taught us to pray to have victory over temptation every day:

Ask a student to read Matthew 6:13, then ask the class: Would the Lord ask us to pray for something that's impossible?

Echoing these words of Jesus, the Anglican Church teaches its members to pray with these words: *"Allow us, O Lord to live this day without sin. Allow us not to fall into sin all day."* In this lesson, we'll study how Jesus Christ responds to that prayer and makes it possible for us to win the battle against the seduction of sin.

Bible Study

1. Live under the control of sin or live in the freedom of the Spirit

The quality of self-control asks us to make a personal decision. The purpose of Jesus' coming to this world was to free us from the dominion of sin. As Jesus' followers, we're responsible for making decisions all the time because we're subjected to trials and temptations every day. If we choose the kind of life that God wants for his children, we must note the following:

Ask two students to read Matthew 5:48 and 1 Peter 1:15.

God commands us to be perfect and holy as He is. However, He doesn't tell us that this will be the result of our self-control, our willpower, the power of our reason over our instincts and desires. The Lord is the one who makes it possible for us to remain in purity. He not only cleanses us of the sins we have done and fills us with the Holy Spirit, but also offers us a life of constant triumph over Satan's attacks.

Purity and maturity are two different things. Purity is the result of the work of the Spirit, removing from our life everything that offends the holiness of God and prevents us from entering his holy presence to have communion with him. Any way in which sin has been established in our lives must be cleansed.

But maturity is the result of a process of growth worked by the Spirit in all areas of our lives. The result is a balanced and holy life, which is also known as maturity. This is the goal of the Christian's life.

But this maturity is not instantaneous, but results from a process of growth. It's a goal that requires investment from us. Time, discipline, constant prayer and life experience, are the tools that will build mature characters. While the quality of self control is developed by the Holy Spirit, nothing can be done without our complete willingness and collaboration, submitting ourselves to this process of being perfected in the likeness of Jesus Christ.

Ask a student to read Mark 7:14-23.

We need the help of the Holy Spirit because simply through our own efforts, we cannot free ourselves from the old chains of our desires that drag us towards what is bad. In this passage, Jesus makes a list of evil desires that have taken root in our hearts and have come to dominate our minds: *"...sexual immorality, theft, murder, adultery, greed, malice, deceit, lewdness, envy, slander, arrogance and folly."*

 Ask students to complete Activity 1.

As we see, many people live under the tyranny of sin. The same happened in the days of Jesus and the Early Church, and that's why the Lord and the apostles over and over again warn about the terrible consequences for the life of a person, a family, a church, or a nation, that has become servants of their unbridled appetites and desires. To be free from the control that sin exercises over our lives, we need to act against the currents of this world. The Spirit will help us, but the decision to live in purity is ours.

2. SELF-CONTROL IN OUR SEX LIFE

Sex is without a doubt the strongest temptation that most people, including Christians, struggle with. Some Christian parents think that it's not wise that their children remain virgins until marriage, that they should have the freedom to enjoy sex with their partners without feeling the guilt of sinning before God. In addition to this, today we have sex education in schools, a formation without Christian values, which promotes individual rights to satisfy appetites without thoughts of any future consequences. In many of our countries, sexual education in schools confuses children and young people, who in their sexual and emotional immaturity doubt their sexual orientation and are encouraged to try various experiences, which confuse them rather than help them, in building healthy self-esteem and identity.

Thank God the Bible is very direct in matters of sexuality, and we're sure that God's norms have not changed. On one occasion, a young man asked a lady pastor what fornication meant in the Bible. She explained that it was all sexual relationships outside the marriage bond between a man and a woman. This young man, who was a student at a seminary, told her that he didn't agree with that definition, that God wouldn't condemn an act of love between two people. As we see, we need to talk and teach more about the practice of sex in our churches, but from the Creator's point of view.

God knew before giving us His laws and commandments the chain of suffering that comes from being driven by desires without control. But Satan has been proactive in spreading the biggest lies about sex, and people have become consumed by their desires. There's no doubt that people's sexual customs have changed a lot in recent decades.

Today, culture is changing at an accelerated pace and with it, values. In many countries, the Bible cannot be taught in schools; they can't even talk about Jesus. But in those same countries, Bibles are distributed in prisons where the gospel is freely preached. Undoubtedly there's a sinister hand behind all these decisions, whose intention is not to help us, or give us freedom, or make us happier, but to lead us on a path of death.

> **Ask students to read and compare Proverbs 16:25 and Proverbs 12:28.**

The Word is very clear: *"This is what the Lord says: See, I am setting before you the way of life and the way of death"* (Jeremiah 21:8). The decision is always ours to believe Satan and his lies about sex and "everything else," or to let the Holy Spirit teach us how to live a balanced life.

Ask students to complete Activity 2.

As we see, there are many challenges that lie ahead in learning to enjoy sexual pleasure within the safe parameters that God has established.

3. How to begin a balanced life?

There are three disciplines that we must practice to begin in a life of self-control.

> **Ask students to see the graph in activity 3: "Disciplines for Self-Control", while developing this lesson point.**

a. Suppress sinful impulses

Sinful impulses are the enemies of the life of holiness since they tempt us to continue with the old ways of thinking, managing emotions, speaking and acting. When we're born again, we're filled with the Holy Spirit, cleansed from our sinful nature, but those old impulses still remain from our past way of living away from Christ.

These tendencies are rooted in us since we acquired them from our family, from society and from our own life experiences. If we don't control them with the help of the Holy Spirit, they'll weaken our resistance to temptation. Isaiah warns us: *"Wash and make yourselves clean. Take your evil deeds out of my sight; stop doing wrong. Learn to do right;..."* (Isaiah 1:16-17).

Let's look at some examples of these tendencies that we must suppress: talking rudely, intolerance, impatience, spreading gossip, judging others, meddling with bad intentions and unhealthy curiosity in the affairs of others, belittling oneself (low self-esteem), evading responsibilities, indebtedness because of wasting money, overeating or eating foods that aren't good for us, neglecting our health, laziness and sedentary lifestyle, wasting time, mental and physical energy in activities that don't do us any good, among others.

b. Plan ways to act differently

The Christian life is a new life; we have to learn to do things differently in the manner of the kingdom of God. The fruit of love and its qualities will help us find new paths for our thoughts, feelings and actions. For this we need to plan strategies in advance in order to be able to resist those bad impulses.

For example, if it bothered us before and filled us with anxiety when there was a lot of traffic, we can plan to take advantage of that time doing something useful, like praying, praising God with music, listening to the audio Bible, recording a list of things to do, etc. If before we were very negative and critical and ready to judge others, we'll need to plan a different way of thinking about people; for example, discover five virtues of each person we know, or say something nice to the person we greet each day, such as: "What a beautiful day the Lord gave us!" Or "I love that sweater you have on today!" Or "How delicious the cake was!"

Transforming habits takes time, but the important thing is to stand firm in the decision to change, have patience as you progress, and appreciate your achievements. These changes will be observed by those who know you and they will be able to recognize the wonderful way in which God is transforming your character.

c. Balance all areas of our lives

We saw that self-control in the Christian's life is not only for the sexual area, but for all areas of life. Some of us have been influenced by fanaticism in our cultures. Fanaticism can be seen in sports, in admiration for famous people, in the defense of a political ideology, of a religion, etc. We have seen how fanaticism provokes violent and obsessive behaviors. People who get carried away by their passions can lose control of themselves, harming themselves and others. Christians need to give up any kind of extreme fanaticism we practiced in our previous lives.

Another area in which we need to learn to discipline ourselves is in the use of time. We must find a time for our personal relationship with God, for Christian service, attending to our responsibilities, taking care of ourselves and our families, without neglecting any of them.

The area of finance is also very important, since an imbalance in our finances will destabilize other areas of our life. To learn to manage what we have with responsibility, we need to resist the consumer culture and the indebtedness that surrounds us. Following the advice of John Wesley will be very helpful: "Earn all you can, save all you can, and give all you can."

Finally, an area that causes many Christians to stumble is that they let problems make them bitter and turn them into resentful and negative people. We cannot avoid having conflicts or disagreements with other people. We cannot control the way other people think, feel and act. But what we can do is face those situations with the help of God's Spirit. There will be conflicts that we cannot "fix," and in those cases instead of hardening our hearts, we have to entrust these people to the Lord and put ourselves forward as peacemakers.

 ....o **Ask students to complete Activity 4.**

 ## Definition of Key Terms

- **Self-control:** It's the control that a person exercises by their will and reason over appetites and thoughts which may lead them to react or act impulsively. Self-control allows for good administration in all areas of life, such as the use of time, managing emotions, financial stewardship, health, relationship management, among others. Synonyms of self-control are: self-discipline, discretion and restraint.

- **Fanaticism:** Passion and excessive tenacity and even without control, acting in defense of beliefs or opinions, especially in sports, religion and politics.

- **Foolishness:** Lack of good judgment or prudence or maturity that's reflected in the way we speak and act. The foolish person despises the advice of the wise or people with more experience, and they act capriciously, guided by their passions and seeking instant gratification of desires, without taking responsibility for the consequences of their actions.

- **Debauchery:** Surrendering to unrestrained enjoyment of pleasures. Mostly it describes sexual pleasures, but it can also be applied to other vices such as alcohol, drugs, violence, among others. Synonyms of debauchery are: dissipation, sexual incontinence, scandal, intemperance, rioting and others.

- **Temperance:** Doing things in moderation. Managing wisely the different areas of life such as finances, time, relationships, health, talents, etc. Synonyms of temperance are: continence, moderation, austerity, self-control, among others.

 ## Summary

The final fruit of love is self-control. The Word teaches us that the Christian's life is one of triumph over temptation and sinful desires and thoughts. Each of the Lord's disciples must learn not to submit to the sinful impulses that can enslave them. For this we need to plan strategies to conduct ourselves differently; how we feel, think, speak and act, in order to reflect the love of God to those around us. For Christians to achieve balance in the different areas of their lives, they must set out on a permanent task of learning and practicing disciplines which will bear fruit for the glory of God.

 **Worksheet**

ACTIVITY 1

Activity to be completed in pairs or in groups of 3 people. The evil thoughts mentioned by Jesus in Mark 7:21-22 are written in the center column below. In the left column, a list of the evil desires that hide behind those sins are included. On the column on the right, write down examples of sinful actions that result from those evil desires and sinful thoughts and that are common in the people of your community.

A Desire that Drives You to do Something	Sinful Thinking	Resulting Conduct, the Sin in Practice
Grudge, Resentment	bad thoughts	
Desire to enjoy sexual pleasure without limitations	adultery	
	fornication	
	lust	
Desire to harm someone	murder	
	slander	
	evil	
Desire to control or dominate others	deception	
	pride	
Desire to have what others have	theft	
	envy	
	greed	
Desire to do what "I want", which gives me pleasure, belittling the wisdom of others.	foolishness	

Worksheet - Lesson 11

ACTIVITY 2
Form three groups and each group answer two of the questions in this activity. Then share your answers with the rest of the class.

a. Does delay in the age of getting married (mostly after age 24) and maintaining courtships for many years help young people resist temptation about sex? What advice would you give a young Christian in this situation?

b. The age to start having sex has decreased. Many teenagers between the ages of 14 and 19 have already had sexual experiences. What can we do as parents and the church to help Christian teenagers wait until marriage?

c. The pregnancies of girls and adolescents increase year by year, with serious consequences for women, children, their families and society as a whole. How can we help our daughters to practice self-control of their sexual desires?

d. In many countries, the struggle for women's rights to abortion without being penalized by law is deepening. When these laws are passed, doctors who work for the government health system cannot refuse to do these procedures. How can we help stop this mass murder of innocent babies? What can a Christian doctor do in the face of this dilemma?

e. How do you think the issue of the danger of pornography should be addressed with youth groups, women and Christian men?

f. How can we protect our children from the malicious gender ideology that confuses their minds and their identities in formation?

ACTIVITY 3
Graph: Disciplines for Self-Control.

ACTIVITY 4
To set goals for your growth towards a mature and balanced life, follow the instructions below.

a. Identify one or two sinful impulses that you need to defeat in your life. Take a minute to pray and ask the Spirit to guide your thoughts before writing.

b. Take a moment to remember how you acted when those impulses dominated you. Then write the strategy you will use in each case to act differently, a way that expresses the holy love of God acting in your life. Before writing, ask God for practical wisdom.

c. Take some time to review your life with the help of the Spirit. Are there areas that are messy? Is there fanaticism that prevails in your life? Are there areas where more balance is needed?

d. What ideas does the Holy Spirit bring to your mind as to what you should do to discipline yourself more are those areas? Write some goals to implement, starting today.

My notes

Worksheet - Lesson 11

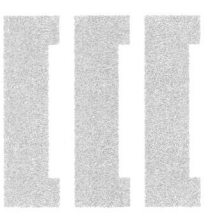
The Fruit of the Spirit in the Church
Lesson 12

Lesson Objectives

That the students might...

- **Understand** that disunity in the church is an evil that needs to be fought against.
- **Learn** to value their lives and love themselves in a balanced way.
- **Make** a commitment to show love for God by serving others.
- **Reflect** on the impossibility of practicing *koinonia* among the people of God without the Fruit of the Spirit.

Visual Aids

- Choose one of these options according to your possibilities:

  A puzzle that has large pieces, like for young children.

  A set of Lego type pieces of different colors, shapes and sizes.

Introduction

One of the challenges that the Church has faced throughout its history is to maintain unity. We often see how Christian churches separate into two congregations because of disagreements between people. This lack of harmony between members is a terrible testimony to the world that observes us.

Unity among the members of a local church won't happen by miracle, nor by magic; unity must be cultivated, work must be done constantly. But why is it so difficult for us to be united as the children of God?

> **Ask students to assemble the puzzle or build a building with the Lego game. Then at the end ask the class: Are all the pieces that we have used the same? In what sense can we see their diversity? What can we learn from this activity regarding the diversity and unity of church members?**

In Latin America, evangelical Christians have grown a lot in recent years, reaching an average of 20 percent of the general population of the region. The Catholic Church has lost its monopoly of more than 500 years since the Spanish conquest. Today, there are more young Hispanics affiliated with the Evangelical Churches than the Roman Catholic Church.

We evangelicals have become an important social force, surpassing in several countries 40 percent of the population (Guatemala, Honduras, Nicaragua). This growth has allowed us to reach leadership positions in the legislature and other areas of public space, reaching high levels of political authority in some countries. But in the midst of all these achievements, divisions still persist.

Big problems challenge us in our communities, countries and regions. To be agents of blessing in our world we have to unite our voices and raise a common front to the evils that beset our peoples. We need as a Church to return to the path of unity and learn to live and serve the world in the Fruit of the Spirit.

In this lesson, we'll study how unity is built in the People of God and how to put into practice the Fruit of the Spirit in our service to the world.

Bible Study

1. THE FRUIT AND UNITY OF THE CHURCH

One of the most important characteristics of the unity of the Church mentioned in the New Testament is the fellowship, or koinonia, among its members. The Greek term koinonia is widely used by Paul in his letters, referring to the fact that Christians should live in communion with each other. Koinonia describes a deep feeling of brotherly love, one that integrates brothers and sisters in the faith of Jesus. This love is the spiritual bond that unites church members.

Ask a student to read Romans 5:5 and ask the class: Where does the love that unites church members come from?

This is a love that comes from God; it's a gift from God for His church, His family. This love must be present in all relationships between church members. It's agape love, a love without selfishness, which by its nature radiates to others. We can affirm that a church without love among its members is not a church born of the Spirit, because the Holy Spirit is love and there's no other way to live in the Spirit, other than a life full of the qualities of God's love.

Ask students to look at the chart in Activity 1.

The following table shows on the left side the ways in which Christians filled with the Holy Spirit relate to each other. Such a church values fellowship, integrates new believers, and resolves their differences and conflicts in a positive way. Believers cultivate friendly relationships and sustain and encourage each other.

The right side of the picture represents the way in which people in a church relate to each other when they are controlled by selfishness. The members of this church need to be filled with the Fruit of the Spirit, a condition of being true sons and daughters of God, and learn to live and serve God in unity.

Ask students to complete Activity 2.

2. THE FRUIT AND ENEMIES OF CHURCH UNITY

A divided church is easily manipulated by Satan. To build unity, we must cast off our pride and put the Fruit of the Spirit into action in our community of faith. How? We can summarize this process in three steps:

Draw the following graph on the board.

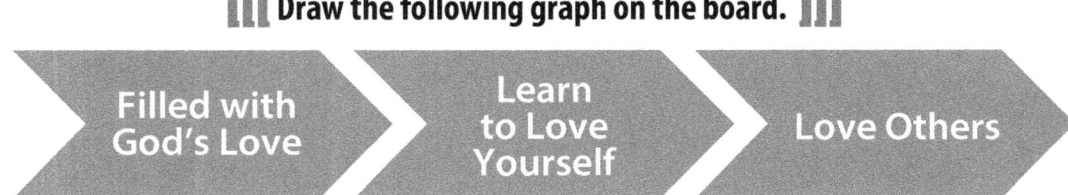

130 *The Fruit-Filled Life*

As we can see in the graph, the first step to being unity builders is to ask God to fill us with the Holy Spirit so that all the qualities of God's love will be developed in our lives. As we saw in the past lessons, if we collaborate with the Spirit, we can see the progressive transformation of our way of thinking, feeling, speaking and acting, according to the model of Jesus.

||| Ask a student to read Romans 12:1-8. |||

In verses 1 and 2 of Romans 12, the apostle Paul describes this experience of complete surrender, which allows our life to make a complete turnabout, being filled with God's love, and living in holiness according to His will. In verse 3, Paul says that while this transformation occurs, there must be a change in the way we think about ourselves. Paul talks about having a balanced concept of the value of our lives.

The society around us doesn't teach us to love ourselves in a balanced way. In the Middle Ages, the theology of pain became popular, which taught that the path to Christian perfection was achieved only through extreme sacrifice and the search for humiliation. It was thought that love for oneself was sin. They considered that there was nothing good in the human being, due to the original sin that dwelt in his flesh. In monasteries and convents, self-flagellation and corporal punishment of one another while praying were common. Called "flagellants," they toured cities making these demonstrations in public.

Even today, there are Christians who practice pilgrimages, strict fasting, sleeping on the ground and other penances, with the purpose of mortifying the body, achieving humility, and submitting the sinful passions of the flesh. It's mistakenly believed that these practices strengthen the human spirit and bring it closer to the suffering Christ, and that the life of holiness is only possible through a life of suffering.

But there's no biblical basis for these self-destructive behaviors, but rather the opposite. In the Old Testament, especially in the Pentateuch, we find many teachings of God to His people about eating a good diet and having healthy habits. Jesus practiced beneficial habits for health, such as exercise and fasting.

 **Ask students to complete Activity 3.**

Loving ourselves in a balanced way means providing our body, mind and spirit with the conditions and sustenance necessary for a healthy life. That's why we must correct any of the extremes into which we may have fallen.

On the one hand, we have people who treat their bodies as if they were trash cans. Many people, even Christians, don't know how to love themselves, and what is worse, they hate each other. They don't treat themselves well, don't maintain good hygiene, don't eat well, don't exercise enough, don't go to the doctor for checkups, don't feed their minds with healthy thoughts, and neglect their emotional and spiritual health.

At the other extreme, we find those who take care of themselves excessively, so that doing so becomes an obsession and an occupation that absorbs all their energies and doesn't allow them to have time to serve God and others. In this group we find those who care too much about taking care of their appearance, but neglect other important areas such as emotional and spiritual life, without which they cannot have a balanced integral health. Neglecting any area of our being is bad stewardship. Excessive care of our body is idolatry, equivalent to worshiping our own image.

The priest and psychologist Jean Monbourquette says that the frequent question that people ask themselves in the psychologist's office is, "Am I worthy enough to be loved?" They are saying that love for themselves depends on the way they look and are valued by others. In other words, they don't feel that they deserve being loved unconditionally.

The greatest experience of love that we can experience in this life is when we discover that God our Creator loves us unconditionally. When we become aware of how valuable our life is to God, we begin to see each other through different eyes. It's an experience that completely transforms us!

The Fruit-Filled Life

We want to be flooded more and more by this love which satisfies that deep thirst for acceptance in each one of us. In this new relationship with the Father, we learn to open ourselves more and more to that love which penetrates all the fibers of our being, healing the wounds left by our past experiences. This love teaches us to make peace with our past and forgive ourselves for all the mistakes we made.

Ask students to complete Activity 4.

It's not possible to build unity in the church without the personal experience of this unconditional love. A person who doesn't love and value himself is unable to love and value others. A healthy self-image is essential to building healthy relationships with other people. That's why we might say that the greatest enemy of unity in the church is a person who doesn't love himself in a balanced way. God's love heals us from low self-esteem and also from self-centeredness, pride and individualism. Experiencing the Lord's healing love is essential to cultivating harmonious relationships with other people. Only when this love, full of grace, floods our being like a river are we able to learn to love ourselves and others with the holy love of God.

3. The fruit and service

In the previous point we saw that when we experience the love of God, we learn to value ourselves and take care of ourselves. This love affirms us and fills us with purpose and energy to love others. On the contrary, when we devalue ourselves, when we have a poor image of ourselves, our gifts and service skills will be wasted. Also, an attitude of haughtiness and pride, of believing ourselves better than others, is equally dangerous.

Ask students to complete Activity 5.

The apostle Paul in Ephesians 2:19-22 compares the Church to a building. Jesus Christ is the one who supports the entire structure, and its foundations are the apostles and prophets. The walls of the lower floors have been built with the lives and service of the Christians who preceded us. The construction work of this building never ends, although with the passage of time the construction materials can change, as well as the construction techniques and the specialties and skills of the workers.

▌▌▌ Ask a student to read Ephesians 2:19-22. ▌▌▌

When the apostle speaks of "church," he doesn't refer to the physical building where we gather to worship, but to the life of all those who make up a local congregation. Paul warns us that for a church to be a holy temple to the Lord, every brick that's inserted must be filled with the fruit of the Holy Spirit. Only then can it fit well into the structure and support the new pieces that will be added in the future. To the extent that the Holy Spirit dwells in every child, youth, adult and elder of the church will the church be "the dwelling place of God in the Spirit." We can see, then, two indispensable requirements for all those who participate in the construction of the church: be filled with the Holy Spirit and work in coordination with others.

There are Christians who are confused about what God expects of them. They deceive themselves by thinking that leading a life of purity, attending church and contributing their tithes and offerings is enough. Christians thus embrace faith selfishly. They treasure all the wonderful works that God has done in their lives, but they don't love others enough to give them a part of their lives. We could call them passive Christians or selfish Christians. James talks about this in his letter:

▌▌▌ Ask a student to read James 2:17. ▌▌▌

For James it was clear that if faith doesn't manifest itself in works of love towards others, it's a hollow faith, a faith that doesn't help us grow in holiness. This sort of faith is not the Fruit of the Spirit. When Christians experience the fullness of the Spirit in their lives, God's love floods their beings and they want to share that love with others. The apostle Peter was also confused about the kind of commitment Jesus expected of him.

> **Read John 21:15-19. Then ask the class:
> How many times did Jesus ask Peter if he loved him?**

In verses 18-19, Jesus tells him: *"Very truly I tell you, when you were younger you dressed yourself and went where you wanted; but when you are old you will stretch out your hands, and someone else will dress you and lead you where you don't want to go."* Jesus said this to imply the kind of death with which Peter would glorify God. After that he added: *"Follow me!"* In other words, Jesus says to him: Peter, it's time that you let me direct you. Give me control of your life! Peter's time of irresponsibility had to come to an end. He needed to start being responsible for others; he needed to mature.

It's not enough to tell God with our words how much we love him; God wants to see our life given to him, serving in His work. Jesus told Peter that he must show his love by serving others in their needs, especially those new to the faith. Peter needed to take another step of faith and make a firm commitment to a life of service.

However, Peter's ministry began on the day of Pentecost when he was filled with the Holy Spirit (Acts 2). It was from that moment on that he embraced the Great Commission of making disciples in the nations. Whatever had slowed him before was pushed aside. Filled with the Spirit, Peter could finally prove that his love for his Lord was deep and true. The work that awaited Peter was difficult, impossible to do without the Fruit of the Spirit. His call was to shepherd, that is to care, exhort, guide, accompany and walk with the new disciples. We know from history that Peter was a great teacher who toured the churches communicating the teachings he had received from Jesus.

Everyone who serves in a ministry to God needs to be filled with the Holy Spirit. The next lesson will broaden this topic.

Definition of Key Terms

- **Self-flagellation:** Act of hurting oneself.
- **Flagellation:** A form of corporal punishment in which scourges are often used (whips, ropes, belts, etc.). It consists of hitting the skin strongly until it destroys it and causes it to bleed.
- **Koinonia:** Greek word used in the New Testament to describe the relationships of fraternal love and fellowship or communion among church members.
- **Penance:** One of the sacraments of the Roman Catholic Church that consists in fulfilling certain acts imposed by the priest after confession of sins. Protestant Churches don't practice this sacrament since the Bible teaches that forgiveness of sins is a free gift from God (Ephesians 2:8-9).
- **Pilgrimages:** A trip that has as its destination a place of importance for the faith of the believer (sanctuary, temple, tomb, among others). It's usually done through long walks that require extreme physical effort. The purpose of this sacrifice may vary between atoning for a sin, attaining grace before God to get any favor, or thanking for any request granted by the divinity. It's practiced by some members of the Roman Catholic Church and other religions, but not by evangelical churches.

Summary

In all times, maintaining unity in the church has been a challenge. *Koinonia* or companionship among the members of the family of God, can only be possible by the work of the Holy Spirit and His gift of love for each of the members. A balanced concept of self is essential to learn to love others, but many people have a distorted idea of the value of their own lives. Only when we understand the Creator's unconditional love for us and open our lives to that love, can we learn to value ourselves in the same way that God does. From this experience that's healing and transformative, we can express our love to others and use our lives in the service of God and others without selfishness.

The Fruit-Filled Life

Worksheet

ACTIVITY 1
Comparative Chart.

A Church filled with the Spirit	A Church filled with Selfishness
Understanding	Intolerance
Sincerity	Hypocrisy
Trust	Distrust
Vulnerability	Defensive
Forgiveness	Hatred
Generousity	Greedy
Active Listening	Desinterest in others
Good Humor, Positive	Bitter, negative
Hopeful	Hopelessness

ACTIVITY 2
Evaluate in groups of 3 to 4 members the fellowship that's currently among the members of your congregation. Mark those characteristics that you observe in your church, the positive and the negative. Then answer the following questions.

a. Look at the negative characteristics you have marked. How can these manifestations of personal pride damage the unity of our church if we don't correct them?

b. Look at the positive characteristics you found. How can these strengths we have in our interpersonal relationships help us overcome the negative aspects we've encountered?

c. Are there people in our congregation who are still struggling with the problem of pride? How can we help them so that they can receive the fullness of the Fruit of the Spirit and learn to relate in love with their brothers and sisters?

ACTIVITY 3
Respond in groups of one to three members.

a. Mention some religious customs that people practice in your context with the purpose of gaining forgiveness or favor from God through personal sacrifice and martyrdom of the body.
   _____

b. Mention some examples of how we can provide our body, mind and spirit with the conditions and sustenance necessary for healthy development.
   _____

Worksheet - Lesson 12

ACTIVITY 4
In groups of two to three people, complete the following prayers, looking in the Bible for some passages that teach us how special, unique and loved we are to God.

- Our integral being is a special _____ of God. God doesn't _____ garbage. (Genesis 1:27 and 5:2)

- We were made a little less than the _____. (Psalms 8:5a)

- We were _____ of His glory. (Ephesians 1:5-6 and Psalms 8:5b)

- He gave us the ability to _____. (Psalms 8:6-8)

- Our bodies are _____ of the Holy Spirit of God that dwells in us. It's part of our worship of God to provide a clean and pleasant place for the Holy Spirit to live. (1 Corinthians 6:19)

- God showed his love for us, while we were still sinners _____. (Romanos 5:8)

- Nothing can _____ from the love of God. (Romans 8:35 and 39)

ACTIVITY 5
In groups of 2 or 3 people answer the following questions.

a. What is the relationship between caring for our health and the service we provide to God and our neighbors?
   _____

b. How does the neglect of our health prevent the Fruit of the Spirit from developing in our lives and being a blessing to others?
   _____

c. How does the neglect of our integral health affect our testimony?
   _____

d. Is there an area where we need to start taking better care of ourselves as of today, to be a more useful instrument in the Lord's work? Write your goals to start this week.
   _____

Worksheet - Lesson 12

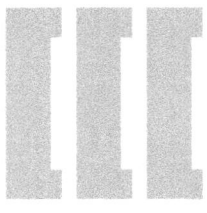
Exercising the Gifts and Fruit of the Spirit
Lesson 13

 **Lesson Objectives**

That the students might...

- **Identify** their misconceptions about gifts.
- **Understand** that gifts are temporary, but the Fruit of the Spirit is forever.
- **Reflect** on the dangers that practicing gifts without love implies for the church.
- **Commit** to serving others in love, joining church ministries.

 **Visual Aids**

- 5 small candles (if they are of varied colors better) and a large tall candle.
- Matches or a lighter.
- A large tray or plate to support the candles and prevent staining the table. The candles should be placed on the tray, the largest one in the center and the small ones around, or on one side the large candle and on the other the small ones.

Introduction

Paul was founding the church in Ephesus (approximately 52 AD) when he received a group of members from the church in Corinth. Their names were Stephanas, Fortunatus and Achaicus (1 Corinthians 16:17). They came to inform him of some problems that were causing disorder in their congregation. One of the problems was competition between them for the use of spiritual gifts, and the confusion they had about their origin and purpose. Paul wrote his first letter to the Corinthians in response to this.

There are still those who confuse the gifts of the Spirit with the Fruit of the Spirit. While it's true that both are gifts that we receive by grace from God, we shouldn't confuse them. That's why we'll complete this study on the Fruit of the Spirit by studying how the qualities of love relate to the exercise of spiritual gifts.

[[[Ask students to complete Activity 1 where they can assess how much they know about spiritual gifts.]]]

Bible Study

1. ORIGIN AND PURPOSE OF SPIRITUAL GIFTS

The Greek word for gift is *charisma*, and for gifts in the plural it's *charismatic*. In its original sense, this word means "gift of God's grace." In the Bible, it's used to indicate special abilities that the Spirit gives to each disciple of the Lord to use in God's service.

Let's see what Paul teaches about the origin and purpose of these gifts or *charismas* that the Spirit distributes:

[[[Read together 1 Corinthians 12:1-11.]]]

In chapter 12, Paul begins by clarifying the origin and purpose of spiritual gifts that the brothers and sisters of the Corinthian church had received. Paul calls them:

"Spiritual" gifts.

Some people get confused when they think that spiritual gifts are natural abilities that come with our DNA, but these gifts aren't abilities with which we're born. Also, they aren't the product of personal intelligence, education, personal effort or experience gained throughout life.

The Fruit-Filled Life

These gifts come from God. In the following graph we can see the commitment of the trinity (verses 4 to 7), each fulfilling their role to provide the church with tools for the mission.

||| Draw this graph on the board. |||

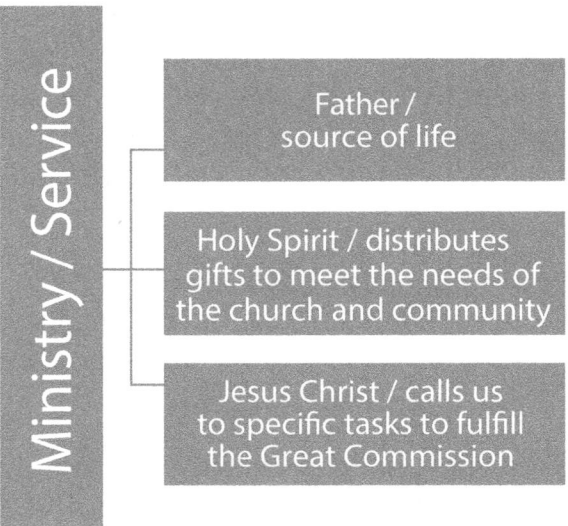

These gifts can be enhanced by our previous experiences. For example, let's think about a person who has studied communication techniques, has a wide vocabulary, knows about education methods and has studied public speaking. Then, when converted, he receives the gift of prophecy (preaching and teaching). His studies and previous experience will enrich his ministry, but none of that background will give him the passion, the power of persuasion, the inspiration and the special charisma that come from the Holy Spirit and that make that gift effective in transforming the lives of listeners.

They are vehicles for God's love to flow.

In the Corinthian Church some were using their gifts to get famous, to be recognized, to gain prestige, respect, authority and a position within the church. Does the same thing happen in some Christian churches today?

In verse 7, Paul affirms that the gifts are manifestations of the Spirit for mutual benefit (1 Corinthians 12:7). That is, the gifts are to benefit others, to meet the needs of others, beginning with our brothers and sisters in the family of faith. The needs of people are quite varied. There are health or material needs, as well as needs of discipleship, advice, guidance, etc.

When we're obedient, the Spirit meets all the needs of His people.

However, in contemporary churches, most of the congregation doesn't get involved in church ministries. Statistics tell us that only 20 percent of the membership participate in ministries inside and outside of the sanctuary, while 80 percent are passive observers.

**||| Ask the class: Does this statistic apply to your church?
Is it possible that the Holy Spirit can meet the needs of the entire congregation when only 20 out of each hundred put their gifts into practice?
How is church for us? Do we go to enjoy the service or
do we go because we want to "serve God"? |||**

Guide the class to complete Activity 2.

They enable us to serve according to our individual call.

The gifts are assigned to each person individually (1 Corinthians 12:7). 1 Corinthians 12:18 says: *"But in fact God has placed the parts in the body, every one of them, just as he wanted them to be."* We cannot choose the gifts, but God chooses us to receive gifts.

Paul mentions more than 20 abilities that the Spirit distributed in the Corinthian church. These are the gifts that the Corinthian Church needed to carry out its ministry.

 **Guide your students to complete Activity 3.**

God in His wisdom knows what each church needs for its service, both for its members as well as for the neighborhood. The gifts also vary according to the times. In his letter to the Corinthians, Paul wrote that that church didn't need any gifts (1 Corinthians 1: 7).

We too can be confident that God will give us all the tools we need for ministry.

Spiritual gifts are distributed among all the members. Each new disciple who joins the congregation receives spiritual gifts when they are born again. That's why new disciples must be incorporated into discipleship as soon as possible so that they can learn the basis of the Christian life and discover their gifts and calling. Then they'll need to be trained to join the ministries of the church.

The only way to combat the passivity we face today in congregations, is by helping people to become true disciples, living in holiness and making a commitment to the ministries of the church.

2. THE GIFTS THAT CAN BE FOUND IN THE CHURCH

To shed more light on this issue, the apostle compares the church to the human body. For Paul, the Church is the body of Christ, a body whose foundation is Jesus Christ, who has also sent us into the world with the mission of extending the kingdom of God through the multiplication of disciples.

This illustration helps us understand the unity that must exist in the church, even in the midst of its diversity, so that it can fulfill the purpose for which it was created. Let's look at some important teachings about how we use spiritual gifts in the church.

Read 1 Corinthians 12:12-31.

a) There are no spiritual gifts that are more important than others

Although some spiritual gifts are more visible than others, all are important for the proper functioning of the body of Christ. There are gifts that are simpler than others, perhaps they aren't as visible, but they are vital to the operation of the church.

Ask the class: In your church, do you consider that some spiritual gifts are more important than others? Which are thought to be more important and which less important? Is it okay for us to make these differences? How do the people you serve feel when they see the "minor" gifts? What would happen to our church if we lacked people with these "less important" gifts?

There are no spiritual gifts better than others, all are necessary. There are no gifts more valuable than others to God and neither should they be for the church. That's why we shouldn't belittle any gift.

Paul says there's no reason to be proud of spiritual gifts since their purpose is not to make us feel more important than others. Spiritual gifts are given to us by grace, not because we deserve them. They shouldn't be used with arrogance or pride, but with a humble attitude. We are servants of the Lord and His church. Pride and arrogance don't come from God, but from Satan.

b) The ministries in the church are to be carried out as a team

In order for the church to fulfill the commission of making disciples of Christ in all nations, all spiritual gifts have to work in coordination towards the same goal. The church is a body on a mission. When each member uses their gifts and abilities, the church can carry out this mission effectively. The image of the body of Christ reminds us that no one spiritual gift is enough to fulfill the needs of such a great mission. We need to work in coordination, complementing each other. In this way the load is distributed and we can do a more excellent job.

The problem is that usually in churches a small group tries to do the work that the entire congregation should do. This small group feels useful, feels fulfilled, feels needed and essential. Although these brothers and sisters may have the best intentions, this isn't the idea of the functioning of the church taught in the New Testament.

> **Ask the class: Let's compare a church with a marriage that has 6 children. In this home, the mother is the one who does all the work and supplies everyone's needs. What could be the consequences for each member of this family in the future? Is this a healthy way to distribute responsibilities?**

There are negative consequences in these church models where the work falls on the shoulders of a few: the leaders become are exhausted and sick, children resent the church or God for depriving them of their parents' attention, the congregation doesn't grow in commitment, there is little expansion of ministry to the community, among others. We need to return to the New Testament church model where each new member is taught to consecrate his or her life in service to the Lord.

Serving in ministerial teams has many advantages. For example:

- It helps us keep pride under control. The fruit of the ministry of a team should be attributed to the team and not to the gifts or effort of a single person (1 Corinthians 12:21).

- It helps us know each other better, cultivate friendships, and support each other (1 Corinthians 12:25).

- It allows us to know what we are really like and how we react in different circumstances, in order to identify the weak areas of our character in which we need to further develop the Fruit of the Spirit.

- We see the most mature Christians in action and learn from their example.

When we serve together, we share our life with our brothers and sisters instead of just greeting each other one day a week. While we serve together, we disciple and are discipled. It's in the midst of the work of the ministry where we build each other up in love (Ephesians 4:1-16).

c) The practice of a spiritual gift without love doesn't edify or build others up.

The problem of the Corinthian church was not the people's lack of commitment, but quite the opposite. Many members used their gifts, albeit in a disorderly way, because they had personal needs. Paul dedicates the whole of chapter 13 to this subject where he comes to the most important question he wants to teach upon.

Ask a student to read 1 Corinthians 13:1-4.

The apostle begins with a list of the gifts which the Spirit had given them and that were central to the ministry of the church. The one he put first, because it was a very precious gift for this church, was the gift of speaking and interpreting foreign languages. This was an essential tool for this multicultural church, especially for teaching and preaching. Then he mentioned the gifts of wisdom and preaching, both necessary for the interpretation and exposition of the Word. He also mentioned faith, but not just any kind of faith, but one that relates to spectacular miracles. Finally, he included generosity and willingness to martyrdom.

Ask the class: If we move these gifts to a contemporary church, we would have good translators, good preachers, ministry of healing and miracles, strong ministry of compassion, and dedicated people who work hard in the ministries, even in the most difficult and dangerous places of the city ... What evaluation would we give to this church? Would we say that their ministries are solid? What qualities does a good leadership team have? What makes a church have the potential to grow in all dimensions?

At first glance, this could be the perfect church; a pastor would be happy to lead such a church. But what has value for God is not what is seen, but the intention of the heart. The Corinthian Church had precious gifts, very valuable for the mission, but they didn't have the most important thing ... they hadn't been filled with the Fruit of the Spirit. When gifts are used without love, they don't edify. Their ministries lacked the power of the Holy Spirit, the only power capable of restoring and transforming people's lives in the likeness of Jesus Christ.

 Ask students to complete Activity 4.

Paul affirms that the exercise of spiritual gifts has a condition: everyone who serves in a ministry for God needs to be filled with the Holy Spirit. God's love leads us to complement each other instead of competing with each other. It's a waste of time, resources and energy when we serve thinking that the church will develop by our ability and talent. The churches are built on the love of Jesus Christ flowing through His servants, not on the talents of a group of people.

The Fruit-Filled Life

3. The most important is everlasting love

In the second part of chapter 13, Paul highlights the virtues or qualities of love as the Fruit of the Spirit. This passage is known as the Love Chapter, and it's a text that's usually read at weddings and applied to relationships. But we must not forget that for Paul, the love of God dwelling in our hearts and flowing from our lives to others is a matter of vital importance in all areas of our life as authentic Christians.

 **Ask students to complete Activity 5.**

In the previous lessons, we studied the beautiful characteristics of the Fruit of the Spirit. Paul adds something else very important about this love.

||| Ask students to read 1 Corinthians 13:8-13. |||

The love of God has no expiration date. Once the Fruit of the Spirit are part of our lives, if we take care of it, it will remain there forever. When we enter into eternal life, either through the experience of death or because the Lord meets us in his Second Coming, the only thing we can take with us will be the fruit of the Holy Spirit. Paul says that the gifts will cease, just as all human works will cease.

||| In this section use candles. While arranging the candles on the tray, explain that the large candle represents the Fruit of the Spirit, the small candles represent the spiritual gifts. Ask students to help light the candles and then guide the discussion with questions like these: Which candles will be extinguished first? If one of these candles represented the duration of our life, which one would we choose? |||

Paul ends this passage by affirming that love is the greatest of all the gifts that the Spirit gives us. The gifts are important for the ministry of the church, but the church cannot exist, nor serve the world, without the Fruit of the Spirit.

The Fruit of the Spirit must be our most precious asset as Christians. Let us choose to live the Christian life in the flow of God's love. May joy and peace flood our inner life; may patience, kindness, goodness and faith be the values that dominate our relationships; may meekness and self-control be the distinguishing features of our character, just as they were in our Lord Jesus Christ.

 Finish the class by following the instructions in Activity 6.

Definition of Key Terms

- **DNA:** This is the acronym for the Deoxyribonucleic Acid Molecule, present in the human body. DNA is the means by which people inherit the characteristics of their ancestors, such as eye color, tone of voice, gestures, height, temperament, etc.

- **Arrogance:** Describes the superior and proud attitude of a person who feels more important than others.

- **Charisma:** Special abilities that God grants as a gift to his sons and daughters for the benefit of the church and the community.

- **Ostentatious:** A person who likes to draw attention to his appearance or behavior. He does things with exaggeration for others to see. He likes to show or pretend that he has money or special talents.

- **Indecorous:** Spoiled, rude, abusive, offends others or makes them feel ashamed.

Summary

In this book we have studied each of the qualities of love as the Fruit of the Spirit. We've seen in this lesson that this fruit of love is indispensable for the exercise of spiritual gifts. All of Christ's disciples are called to be actively involved in the ministry of the church. Ministry is the purpose for which the Father gives us life, the Spirit gives us abilities, and Jesus Christ calls us to a specific task. When we're obedient and respond to this call, the Lord supplies all the needs of His people. However, for our ministries to bear the fruit expected by God, we need to be filled with the Fruit of the Spirit.

 **Worksheet**

ACTIVITY 1
Mark the following sentences that you consider to be true with a "T" and those that are false with an "F". After the Bible study at the end of the lesson, you can review your answers and correct the wrong answers.

__ Christians shouldn't use their spiritual gifts without the Fruit of the Spirit.

__ Spiritual gifts will endure into eternal life.

__ Spiritual gifts are abilities we're born with.

__ Jesus Christ calls each of us to a special task in his kingdom.

__ In a healthy church, 20 percent use their gifts.

__ Without spiritual gifts, the church has no ministerial tools.

__ Some spiritual gifts are more important than others.

__ All churches need the spiritual gift of tongues (languages).

__ Working in ministerial teams edifies us.

__ The Fruit of the Spirit will endure into eternal life.

ACTIVITY 2
Answer the following questions.

a. What are the gifts of the Spirit that you have been able to identify in your life?

_____
_____

b. How can you put these gifts into practice in order to help the integral development of your church? Mention some examples.

_____
_____

c. How can the Holy Spirit bless the people of your community through these special gifts He has given you? Mention some examples.

_____
_____

Worksheet - Lesson 13

ACTIVITY 3
In groups of 3 to 4 members, complete in the chart the lists of gifts that Paul makes to different churches in his letters. Then compare them and see if there are differences.

The Church in Corinth 1 Corinthians 12:8-10	The Church in Ephesus Ephesians 4:11	The Church in Rome Romans 12:6-8

ACTIVITY 4
Below is a list of three gifts that are practiced in almost all congregations. Evaluate each gift by answering the questions.

	Teaching-Preaching	Generosity	Faith
What qualities of love, Fruit of the Spirit, are indispensable for this gift to build the church?			
What are the dangers of using this gift without love for the church?			
What evidence should we expect from this gift when used with love?			
What gifts are complementary to this gift?			

Worksheet - Lesson 13

ACTIVITY 5

In groups of three to four, read 1 Corinthians 13:4-7. Then verify that the lists below are complete. If you need to clarify the meaning of a term, you can use a dictionary or an internet search engine.

What:

- Is patient

- Is kind

- Rejoices in the Truth

- Always protects

- Always trusts (has faith in people)

- Always hopes

- Always perseveres

What:

- Isn't jealous

- Isn't ostentatious (vain)

- Isn't arrogant (proud)

- Doesn't dishonor others

- Isn't self-seeking (selfish, greedy)

- Isn't easily irritated (angry, treats others harshly)

- Doesn't keep track of wrongs (of the mistakes of others)

- Doesn't enjoy injustices (when someone else is doing something evil)

ACTIVITY 6

Below are two lists with some "attitudes" that people have when we use spiritual gifts with love or without love. Evaluate your own life and mark those attitudes that are present in you. Then write your goals to put into practice the qualities of love, which is the Fruit of the Spirit, in your service as of today.

Attitudes that accompany the use of spiritual gifts without love:

__ Feel offended if you aren't thanked for your work.

__ Critically criticizes others for their "imperfections."

__ Think you're the best at what you do.

__ If you aren't the leader, you prefer not to work.

__ Are happy when others make mistakes.

__ Get angry if things aren't done your way.

__ Get annoyed when someone else gets the credit.

__ Like to be the center of attention.

__ Are impatient with people who make mistakes.

__ You feel offended if you're assigned humble tasks.

__ See ministry as an obligation.

Attitudes that accompany the use of gifts as Fruit of the Spirit

__ Have faith in people.

__ Have the patience to train others how to use their spiritual gifts.

__ Rejoice when others use their spiritual gifts well.

__ Work as a team, valuing the gifts of others.

__ Are pleased to serve with younger or less experienced people.

__ Congratulates others for their work.

__ Serve with joy and enthusiasm.

__ Feel that serving is a privilege, not an obligation or a burden.

__ Do not mind doing humble tasks.

__ Strive to do the best for God.

MY GOALS:

_____
_____
_____
_____
_____
_____

Bibliography

Barclay, William (1972-1974) *New Testament Commentary.* John II (volume 6), Mathew I & II (Volume 1 & 2) & Luke (Volume 4). Buenos Aires: La Aurora.

Bayley, Kenneth (2013) *Paul Through Mediterranean Eyes.* Nashville, Tennessee: Nelson Group.

Belch, Carlos (1998). *Hidden Treasures. Grammatical and explanatory commentary on Romans*, 1 Corinthians & 2 Corinthians. London, USA. Evangelical Publications.

Duewel, Wesley L. (2000). God offers you his great salvation. Nappanee, Indiana: Evangel Publishing House.

Kenneson, Philip (2004). *Life on the Vine: Cultivating The Fruit of the Spirit in Christian Community.* Buenos Aires: KAIROS.

Purkiser, W.T., Taylor, R., Taylord, W. (s/f) *God, Man & Salvation.* Kansas City, Missouri: NPH.

Schwarz, Christian (2004) *The 3 Colors of Love.* Barcelona: CLIE.

Semana-Tendencias. (3/3/2018) *En las manos de Dios los evangélicos conquistan las urnas en América Latina.(In the hands of God the evangelicals conquer the polls in Latin America)* Consultado 9 de febrero de 2019 de: https://www.semana.com/mundo/articulo/candidatos-presidenciales-que-son-evangelicos-y-cristianos-en-america-latina/558919

Silva-Silva, D. (2005) *El fruto eterno. Pequeña semilla-árbol frondoso. (The eternal fruit. Small leafy seed-tree)* Miami, Fl: CLIE.

Wilkinson, Bruce. (1998) *Personal holiness in times of temptation.* Miami: Unilit.

www.ingramcontent.com/pod-product-compliance
Lightning Source LLC
Chambersburg PA
CBHW081346040426
42450CB00015B/3322